"A clear vision gives an organization heart. Without it, work will have no meaning. *Full Steam Ahead!* is a must read."

—James H. Amos, Jr., Chairman Emeritus, Mail Boxes Etc.

"Before beginning any kind of planning, everyone on the team should read this book. It will ensure you're headed in the right direction. *Full Steam Ahead!* should be required reading."

—Barbara Bennett, Former Executive Vice President, The Stanley Works

"Leadership is about going somewhere. Without a clear vision your leadership doesn't matter. *Full Steam Ahead!* will help your leadership efforts get started in the right direction."

—James E. Despain, Former Vice President, Caterpillar and author of *And Dignity for All*

"Great things come from a powerful vision—fortunes are made, diseases get cured, and democracies are born. Blanchard and Stoner not only teach readers how to develop a potent vision in *Full Steam Ahead!*, but also how bring it alive in the hearts and minds of people who will make it happen."

—Robert W. Jacobs, author of *Real Time Strategic Change*

"Blanchard and Stoner demonstrate how clear vision helps you focus on the results you desire. Time is a precious commodity. *Full Steam Ahead!* shows you how to get the most out of your efforts."

—Loyal Nordstrom, President, Honolulu Holdings Inc.

Full Steam Ahead!

FULL STEAM AHEAD!

Unleash the
Power of Vision in Your Company
and Your Life

Ken Blanchard
Jesse Stoner

BERRETT-KOEHLER PUBLISHERS, INC.
San Francisco

Berrett-Koehler Publishers, Inc.
235 Montgomery, Suite 650
San Francisco, CA 94104-2916
Tel: (415) 288-0260   Fax: (415) 362-2512   www.bkconnection.com

ORDERING INFORMATION

Quantity sales. Special discounts are available on quantity purchases by corporations, associations, and others. For details, contact the "Special Sales Department" at the Berrett-Koehler address above.

Individual sales. Berrett-Koehler publications are available through most bookstores. They can also be ordered direct from Berrett-Koehler: Tel: (800) 929-2929; Fax: (802) 864-7626; www.bkconnection.com

Orders for college textbook/course adoption use. Please contact Berrett-Koehler: Tel: (800) 929-2929; Fax: (802) 864-7626.

Orders by U.S. trade bookstores and wholesalers. Please contact Publishers Group West, 1700 Fourth Street, Berkeley, CA 94710. Tel: (510) 528-1444; Fax (510) 528-3444.

Production management: Michael Bass & Associates

Berrett-Koehler and the BK logo are registered trademarks of Berrett-Koehler Publishers, Inc.

Printed in the United States of America

Berrett-Koehler books are printed on long-lasting acid-free paper. When it is available, we choose paper that has been manufactured by environmentally responsible processes. These may include using trees grown in sustainable forests, incorporating recycled paper, minimizing chlorine in bleaching, or recycling the energy produced at the paper mill.

Library of Congress Cataloging-in-Publication Data
Blanchard, Kenneth H.
    Full steam ahead!: unleash the power of vision in your company and your life / by Ken Blanchard, Jesse Stoner.
        p. cm.
    ISBN 1-57675-244-5 (alk. paper)
    1. Goal (Psychology) 2. Planning. 3. Business planning 4. Mission statements. I. Stoner, Jesse, 1949– II. Title.
    BF505.G6 .B53 2002
    650.1—dc21
                                                        2002038319
                                                        CIP

First Edition
06 05 04 03   10 9 8 7 6 5 4 3 2 1

Dedicated to my children, Michael and Noah

—JESSE STONER

my grandchildren, Kurtis and Kyle

—KEN BLANCHARD

*who have brought dimension
to our own personal visions*

Contents

Preface

Vision creates focus. Vision identifies direction. Vision unleashes power. Vision allows you to move *Full Steam Ahead!*

The expression *full steam ahead* comes from the days of steamships when it meant the powerful ships were moving ahead full force. Today, *full steam ahead* means being so clear about your purpose, so committed to it, so sure about its importance, and so sure about your ability to accomplish it, that you are able to take decisive action despite obstacles. In our book this expression describes the effect of having a clear vision—knowing who you are, where you're going, and what will guide your journey—fully powered to move ahead full force. In order for organizations to be fully powered, the leaders need to know how to create a compelling vision that resonates with the hopes and dreams of those in the organization. Leadership is about going somewhere. If not in service of a shared vision, leadership can become self-serving.

In our work with organizations worldwide, we realized that the biggest impediment blocking most managers from being great leaders was the lack of a clear vision for them to serve. Less than 10 percent of the organizations we visited had a clear purpose, a set of operating values, or a picture of the future. In other words, they didn't have a clear sense of where they were trying to lead people.

Most of the people we talk with agree that vision is important. They know that without a clear vision, they are inundated with demands for their time that can get them off focus and waste a lot of energy. They recognize the negative effect of lack of vision, but they are also unsure of how to create one.

In many organizations where a vision statement does exist, it turns people off. It may be found framed on walls but provides no guidance or, worse, has nothing to do with the reality of how things actually are.

If you have never had a vision or have participated in a failed effort at creating one, this book can help you succeed now. We have taken this seemingly complex subject and translated it so that it is simple to understand, down-to-earth, and easily applied.

Full Steam Ahead! takes the mystery out of the "vision thing." It makes vision accessible to everyone, in both their organizations and their personal lives. It explains the three key elements of a compelling vision and how to create a shared vision that unleashes energy and potential. The process described in our book connects with your business and its business objectives; it's not just a "feel good" process. Our book shows what happens to businesses and individuals that don't have a clear vision—the financial, operational, and personal implications of an unclear vision. It demonstrates how these concepts can be applied in a variety of ways: creating a vision for a company, for a department, for a family, and for one's personal life. And it will give you some ideas on what to do right now.

The information presented in our book comes from the culmination of over twenty years of study and experience in facilitating the process of creating a shared vision within diverse fields, including manufacturing, resorts, automotive, public relations, retail, health care, government, education, other nonprofit, and communities. We have received as much from the people in these organizations as we have given, and as a result we have improved the process based on the lessons learned over the years.

This book is about more than how to create a compelling vision. It's also about how to ensure that it's a shared vision, it comes alive, and it continues to guide you on a day-by-day basis. Creating a vision statement can be just a one-time activity. This book is about how to make visioning a journey.

Our hope for you, the reader, is that you get some practical ideas on how to create a vision—for your organization or department, for your work, and for your life. The lessons are embedded throughout the book, like nuggets waiting to be discovered.

We hope you enjoy reading this book and discovering the lessons as much as we enjoyed writing it. And we hope that you are able to apply the concepts in this book so you can move full steam ahead!

KEN BLANCHARD

JESSE STONER

Spring 2003

Without a Good-bye

I stood in disbelief, unaware of the wind that lashed across my face. Lost in my thoughts, I was numb to the cold. *I can't believe he's gone . . . I can't believe I never got to say good-bye.* I couldn't imagine a world without Jim in it. Yet, here I stood at an open grave on this gloomy winter day.

How can this be happening? I wondered. I had believed that Jim would always be there if I needed him. Now I needed him—to comfort me—and he wasn't there. I wanted desperately to talk to him.

I looked around at those gathered with me. They looked as shocked as I felt. Jim had meant so much to all of us. I gathered some comfort as I realized I was not alone.

As Jim's daughter Kristen read the eulogy, I began to listen closely to what she said. The familiar words described Jim so well that I could almost sense his presence. Feeling that connection with Jim, I realized that I felt alone but not lonely. Alone, yet, I could almost feel Jim comforting me.

"Jim Carpenter was a loving teacher and example of simple truths, whose leadership helped himself and others awaken the presence of God in their lives. He was a caring child of God, a son, brother, spouse, father, grandfather, father-in-law, brother-in-law, godfather, uncle, cousin, friend, and business colleague, who strove to find a balance between success and significance. He had a spiritual peace about him that permitted him to say no in a loving manner to people and projects that got him off purpose. He was a person of high energy who was able to see the positive in any event or situation. No matter what happened, he could find a 'learning' or a message in it. Jim Carpenter was someone who trusted God's unconditional love and believed he was truly the beloved. He valued integrity, his actions were consistent with his words, and he was a mean, lean, 185-pound, flexible golfing machine. He will be missed because wherever he went, he made the world a better place by his having been there."

A loving teacher and example of simple truths. I reflected on how eloquently the words of the eulogy described how Jim had lived his life. They captured the essence of who he was. I smiled to myself as I thought about how the words had even captured Jim's humor. He certainly loved golf, even though he had never become a "mean, lean golfing machine."

As we walked away from the cemetery, I caught up with Kristen.

"That was a lovely eulogy," I told her as I put my arm around her.

Kristen sighed and said, "Thanks, Ellie. But I didn't write it. I think Dad did. I was sitting at his desk in his study, trying to compose a eulogy when I found this one lying in the top drawer. I thought it described him better than anything I could have written."

She paused a moment and continued, "But I don't know *why* he would have written it."

Then it hit me why the words had sounded so familiar.

"I know why," I replied softly. "I was there, when he wrote it. It was his vision for his life."

Immediately my thoughts flew back to another winter ten years earlier, which had started not unlike this one.

An Unfamiliar World

Gray skies prevailed that winter. It hardly snowed, but a chill settled deep and we rarely saw the sun. I felt numb as I stood uncertainly at the threshold of an unfamiliar world. I was in my midthirties. My husband had walked out on me—on our marriage, our children, and our life. One morning he announced that he was leaving, and that afternoon, he was gone.

I was shattered. I couldn't believe I hadn't seen it coming. I felt stupid as I put the signs together that I had missed. Over the past few years I had been so involved with the children and managing our busy lives, it had barely registered that Doug had become more distant. I thought he was busy at work.

The divorce happened quickly. My lawyer assured me I was getting a good settlement. He said, "Doug is cooperating because he feels guilty." But it still wasn't enough money for us to live on. I had to get a job but had no idea where to start. My job to that point in my life was to be a mother, a wife, and a volunteer, not earn money to support the family. It seemed as if all the things I had taken for granted were over.

My children were teenagers now and didn't need me in the same way they once had. I felt totally alone and overwhelmed. There were days when just getting out of bed felt like a major accomplishment. I kept running out of steam.

Finally, a practical voice from somewhere inside said *Take it one step at a time.* I knew the first thing I needed to do was find a source of income. I considered my situation. I was intelligent. I had graduated at the top of my class. I had been treasurer of our children's PTA. I did bookkeeping for the library auxiliary. I paid our bills (on time!) and did our taxes. I also loved to write, but who could earn a living as a writer when she's had no formal training? My degree was in business.

I anxiously perused the classified ads for a business or financial position each Sunday as I wallowed in misery. And so eventually, I found my first job—in the accounting department of a good-sized insurance agency. I went shopping for business clothes and prepared to enter this strange new world.

• • •

My first day on the job went better than I had expected. A friendly woman named Marsha—who had interviewed me for the position—welcomed me to the agency and confirmed that I would report to her. She showed me around the department, gave me a tour of the building, and outlined my responsibilities. My specific responsibilities were to support tax accounting—collect tax-related information and help prepare the state and federal reports.

She said that I would begin slowly until I got into the swing of things, which was reassuring. I sensed that my life was about to be dredged out of the murky swamp in which I had sunk. In fact, I was actually excited to learn my responsibilities, meet my co-workers, and get my own cubicle along with my own desk, my own computer, and my own voicemail box. There was even a message waiting for me on voicemail:

Good morning, everyone. This is Jim. It's said that Abraham Lincoln often slipped out of the White House on Wednesday evenings to listen to the sermons of Dr. Finnes Gurley at New York Avenue Presbyterian Church. He generally preferred to come and go unnoticed. So when Dr. Gurley knew the president was coming, he left his study door open.

On one of those occasions, the president slipped through a side door in the church and took a seat in the minister's study, located just to the side of the sanctuary. There he propped the door open, just wide enough to hear Dr. Gurley.

During the walk home, an aide asked Mr. Lincoln his appraisal of the sermon. The president thoughtfully replied, "The content was excellent; he delivered with elegance; he obviously put work into the message."

"Then you thought it was an excellent sermon?" questioned the aide.

"No," Lincoln answered.

"But you said that the content was excellent. It was delivered with eloquence, and it showed how hard he worked," the aide pressed.

"That's true," Lincoln said, "But Dr. Gurley forgot the most important ingredient. He forgot to ask us to do something great."

I believe there is nothing wrong with average lives and average accomplishments; most of the good of the world builds on the accumulated efforts of everyday people. But a life should strive for greatness, as Lincoln seemed to know.

I remember that voicemail message quite accurately—because I actually transcribed it. I didn't have much to do my first morning, and I thought it would provide good practice for my computer skills. Besides, the message intrigued me. Who was Jim, and why was his message in my voicemail box? This was something I hadn't expected in the business world.

Marsha invited me to lunch, along with others on her staff. We chatted about an upcoming big project, the weather, and our families. I began to think that I would actually like working for this company. It felt comfortable. I wanted to be here. I hadn't felt like this since long before Doug left us.

I didn't ask about the voicemail message partly because it slipped my mind and mostly, frankly, because I didn't want to sound as if I didn't know about the business world.

The afternoon went by quickly, and I headed home feeling hopeful about my future for the first time in a long time.

• • •

The next few days, I dug right in. I was eager to learn everything as quickly as possible so I'd be viewed as an asset. By Friday, I still hadn't asked anyone about the voicemail messages. But each morning, I was intrigued by the brief message that began with the words "Good morning, everyone. This is Jim." And, each day, when I had extra time, I transcribed the message—mostly so I would look busy if someone passed by my cubicle.

The messages were quite unusual. They seemed to be a mix of stories, personal philosophy, and information about things that were happening in people's lives. For example, one message began:

Good morning, everyone. This is Jim. Yesterday Sue Mason, one of our receptionists, had a successful operation, but they did find some cancer. They think they got most of it out, but she's got to go through some chemotherapy. So let's send our prayers, good energy, and positive thoughts toward Sue.

I hadn't met Sue, but I sent her some positive thoughts anyway. I felt it couldn't hurt. I still hadn't asked anyone about the messages, partly because it never seemed to be the right time to do so. And partly because it had become a bit of a mystery—something to look forward to each day. It had been a long time since I had some mystery in my life.

When I got home at the end of my first week of work, I reflected on my experiences. I had been excited and anxious most of the week. Work felt a little stressful, but not nearly as stressful compared to the dreariness of home. All the energy I had at work disappeared the moment I walked in the house. Alex and Jen were at their father's for the weekend. Even when they were around, they seemed so self-sufficient. At the ages of fifteen and thirteen, they made their own plans, and, as far as I could tell, all they needed me for was transportation. Once I had been a wife and a mother. Now I wasn't sure who I was. I slept late both Saturday and Sunday and moped around feeling useless, waiting for Monday to roll around.

Out of the Gloom

By Sunday night, I truly looked forward to getting out of the gloom of the dreary weekend and going back to work. The problem was I couldn't sleep. After a fitful night, I woke up at 5:30 A.M. and lay in bed. I tried to fall back asleep, with no success. What to do? Alex and Jen had slept at their father's. The thought of getting up and facing the empty house was unappealing. I considered going into work early. Thinking about work, I began to feel more energy. I had been assigned a project. If I did a good job, it might prove my capabilities. *Why not get at it?* I thought. I dressed quickly and arrived at work around 6:30 A.M.

It hadn't occurred to me that the building would be locked. Walking around the building, I tested the doors and found one unlocked in the back. I entered the quiet building with a bit of trepidation. I hadn't met many of the people who worked there yet, and I didn't want to be arrested for breaking and entering.

The door opened into a hallway, and I was immediately drawn to the aroma of freshly brewed coffee coming from a room to my left. I vaguely noticed several photocopy machines and, to my delight, found the fresh coffee in a large coffeemaker on the counter at the entrance to the room. It smelled so wonderful that I walked over and helped myself to a cup. I started to relax and feel pleased with myself, when suddenly, I heard a "humpf" behind me. Startled, I turned and spilled my coffee. I hadn't noticed a small table almost hidden in the back of the room behind the copy machines, nor had I noticed the man sitting at it. But clearly he had noticed me. He sat comfortably with a cup of coffee and appeared to have been watching me for some time. Was that a smug look of self-satisfaction? I had seen that look on Doug's face many times when he caught me making a mistake.

I came back on the offensive. "Who are you? Why didn't you tell me you were here? I could have burned myself when you startled me!"

He responded, "Are you OK?" He sounded sincere. I looked at him again. Actually, his smile wasn't really smug. And, he had the most striking blue eyes I had ever seen. They seemed to see right through me—right through my blustery surface.

"Care to join me?" he invited.

I sheepishly wiped up the spilled coffee and joined him.

"I'm new here," I explained apologetically. "I wanted to come in early to get some work done, and this was the only door open."

I thought he might be a custodian or a security guard, but somehow it didn't matter who he was. I immediately felt so comfortable in his presence that I just opened up. I told him about my failed marriage. The shock that Doug had been having an affair for three years with our neighbor Diane. How he left us. How my kids didn't seem to need me. How I had started in my position last week. I told him how I was nervous about my first real job and that I was eager to learn quickly. I talked about being a mother, a volunteer at my children's schools, and my utter lack of a social life. I must have jabbered nonstop for twenty minutes.

It suddenly occurred to me that I was being rude. I hadn't asked him anything about himself. I didn't even know his name. "Forgive me. You're such a good listener that I've monopolized the conversation, and I don't even know your name."

His blue eyes looked me over, and he grinned. "My name is Jim, and I'm the president of the agency. I enjoyed meeting you, Ellie, and learning about your very full life. And now, if you'll excuse me, it's time for me to get to work." He stood up and walked off, leaving me stunned and speechless.

Later that morning, when I listened to my voice-mail, I heard the following message:

 Good morning everyone, this is Jim. It's a little after 7:00. I was talking with Ellie, our new associate in the accounting department, this morning and I was reminded of a story I'd like to share with you.

One day an expert in time management was speaking to a group. He pulled out a one gallon, wide-mouthed jar and set it on the table in front of him. He also produced about a dozen fist-sized rocks and carefully placed them, one at a time, into the jar. When the jar was filled to the top and no more rocks would fit inside, he asked, "Is this jar full?"

Everyone said "yes."

He then reached under the table and pulled out a bucket of gravel. He dumped some gravel in and shook the jar, causing pieces of gravel to work themselves down into the spaces between the rocks. He then asked the group once more, "Is the jar full?"

But this time some of the group was not so sure.

"Good," he said as he reached under the table and brought out a bucket of sand and dumped it in the jar. Once more he asked the question, "Is the jar full?"

No one answered.

He then grabbed a pitcher of water and poured it in until the jar was filled to the brim. He looked at the class and asked, "What's the point of this illustration?"

One bright young man said, "The point is, no matter how full your schedule is, if you really think about it, you can always fit more things in it."

"No," the speaker replied with a smile. "That's not the point. That's what most people think. The truth this illustration teaches is that if you don't put the big rocks in first, you'll never get them in at all."

What are the big rocks in your life? Time with your loved ones, your dreams, your health, a worthy cause? Remember to put these in first or you'll never get them in at all.

So, one part of the mystery was solved. The voice-mail messages came from Jim, the company's president. Although I now knew who was leaving the messages, I still didn't know why.

I kept my questions to myself and hurried through another busy day without thinking further about the remaining mystery or the message.

That night as I lay in bed, I thought about what the big rocks were in my life. My children, certainly. And my new job. What else? I drifted off with images of rocks surrounding me—and I was stuffed in a jar with them.

• • •

Tuesday, I again awoke at 5:30 and hopped out of bed. This time I knew exactly what I was going to do. The evening before, I had asked Alex and Jen whether they would mind if I left for work before they left for school. So, I woke them up, put cereal on the table for their breakfast, and arrived at the office at about 6:30. I wondered whether Jim would be there. I tested the back door, and it opened. I walked directly to the copy room, and there he was, sitting quietly at the table. I studied him more carefully this time. He was an attractive man, lean—an athlete, maybe, when he was younger. His thinning blonde hair and fine, crinkled lines around his eyes gave a hint that he might be in his early fifties. The most noticeable thing about his appearance was the intensity of his blue eyes. Once I started looking into them, it was almost impossible to look away.

He didn't seem surprised to see me and said, "Good morning, Ellie. You're early again today. Want to tell me more?" he invited with a smile.

"Nope," I replied. "This time I've got some questions for you."

I plunged right in. "Why do you leave a voicemail message every morning? How long have you been doing it? What do you want to accomplish? How do you keep thinking of new things to say? Do you get tired of doing it?"

"Whoa!" Jim responded. "You weren't kidding yesterday when you said you were eager to figure things out quickly."

We both laughed as I poured myself a cup of coffee.

Again I felt so at ease. On one hand, I knew he was the president of the company, and that meant I should probably have been intimidated or in awe of him. But there was something real and human about him that made me feel like he was a "normal" person. Maybe it was the ease of the early morning hours or the way I had opened up to him before I knew who he was. In any case, I just felt comfortable with him. And I liked him!

I sat down across from him and waited.

After a moment Jim laughed and said, "OK, I get it. Now it's my turn to talk. Those are good questions. But I'm not sure I have all the answers you want."

He continued, "I left the first message about a year ago. A woman named Alice, who had started with the agency when my father was president, had just gotten married. A week later her new husband, Tom, was diagnosed with a malignancy and had to go in for surgery. As you can imagine, she was distraught. And I felt terrible. I had participated in their wedding and had known Alice for years. The day before the surgery she asked me to send my prayers for Tom. I was happy to do that, because that was what Alice wanted me to do. Then I thought, 'Why just me—why not everyone?' The next morning I left a voicemail message for everyone and asked them to send their prayers, good thoughts, and energy in Tom's direction. I had no idea what kind of an impact that would have on Alice or on the agency. I just thought it was a good thing to do. Alice called me in tears the next day. The surgery had gone well. She was crying because she was so touched by the message I had left and all the responses she had gotten as a result. Her voicemail box was full. And my voicemail was filled with messages from people saying how wonderful my message was. I thought, 'I'm onto something here.'

"We had been growing so fast as a company that no one knew the important stuff going on in one another's lives. By leaving that voicemail message company-wide, I was able to help us regain something of a small company feeling."

"So your messages helped keep people connected with each other?"

"Yes, I guess you might say that. But I think there's more. I also saw how they created energy and a sense of community," Jim replied thoughtfully as he searched to put his thoughts into words. "I feel like these messages are making a difference even though I'm not sure how. I think they're good for the agency and good for me."

"How are the messages good for you?" I asked.

"Well, if I'm going to leave a message every morning, I have to spend some time thinking about what's important. I need to compose my thoughts and focus. I used to jump out of bed in the morning and hit the pavement running. Leaving these messages forces me to slow down a bit before I speed up."

"Personally, I think it sets a nice tone for the day. I've been . . . ," I began and then hesitated as I immediately felt foolish. I had almost mentioned that I had been transcribing his messages.

Jim smiled at me kindly and laughed. "Your questions and views are refreshing. And I would like to talk with you more. But now it's time for me to get going."

I looked at my watch and was amazed! I couldn't believe how quickly the time had flown by.

I went to my cubicle and began working on my project. Later that morning when I checked my voicemail, there it was—Jim's message for the day. It began:

Good morning, everyone. This is Jim.

    Leaving you these morning messages has really helped because so often I'm tempted to race out of bed, jump into my task-oriented self, get on the phone, start writing, doing all kinds of tasks. When I do that, suddenly my day takes off, and it's out of my control. Leaving these messages forces me to think about what's important before I jump into my day.

I was fascinated by this message. I had met with Jim on two occasions, and a part of both conversations were woven into his morning messages.

The "Vision Thing"

Wednesday, I arrived precisely at 6:30 A.M. There was Jim at the back table. It almost seemed as if he were waiting for me. He immediately began talking as though yesterday's conversation had just occurred.

"I knew I was onto something with the tremendous response I had gotten from my first voicemail message. I'll tell you a story, so you'll see what I was looking for.

"Once there was a successful manager who was pretty effective in traditional ways. He set clear goals, and people knew what they were being asked to do. He tended to manage by wandering around. He caught people doing things right and praised them. And if they were off base, he would redirect them or sometimes even reprimand them when they knew better. People liked to work for him. And they respected him. But as he looked in his own heart, he felt that something was missing. And when he looked in the eyes of his people, he saw that they were enjoying what they were doing. But they didn't seem to have that sparkle that he had seen when he was a young man when they all worked for a leader who inspired them and made them feel that what they were doing was really important. Back then, every day he walked by, early in the morning and late into the evening, people were working—not because they had to but because they wanted to. They were enjoying what they were doing, and they had something special. Now, this manager felt that the magic and energy weren't there. And he was wondering what was missing and what he could do that would ignite himself and other people even more. Then one day, he left a powerful voicemail message, and he knew he was onto something."

I listened intently to his story. "So, that manager was you, right?"

Jim nodded. "And the inspiring leader was my father."

"Your father?"

"My father was an amazing man. He started this agency from nothing—sheer guts, loans, and a belief in people. He built it into the thriving, well-respected business it is today. Everyone adored my father—the employees, our customers, especially the widows! They wanted our agency to succeed, and they made it sparkle. I was proud to work my way up through the ranks. I took the helm a little over ten years ago when he retired. Unfortunately, I didn't have much time to get his guidance before he died. We're doing well financially, but I haven't had the significant impact I have wanted. Now I'm hoping these messages might be a way to help accomplish that."

I thought a moment. "So, you're the president of a successful, respected agency. When your father was president, things sparkled. Now people seem happy, but the sparkle isn't there. You feel like you are a good manager, but there must be something more, and you don't know what it is."

"That about sums it up," he replied.

"It also sounds like it's not that exciting or fulfilling for you, either," I ventured, knowing I was pushing our conversation further than he might want.

Jim laughed heartily. "Ellie, I don't know how you get the courage to speak up like that. But I'll be honest with you. You're absolutely right. I like it here, but I'm not excited to be here."

I smiled back. If Jim saw it as "courage," that was great. My mother used to say my mouth was like a gumball machine—whenever I started to talk, you never knew what was going to come out. It got me into trouble with some people. But it didn't seem to faze Jim.

• • •

Thursday morning, Jim and I were again drinking coffee at "our" table.

"You know, Ellie, I've been thinking about your questions about my messages. I can sense that they're making some sort of an impact, but as I said yesterday, I still don't feel that the significant shift I've been hoping for has taken place.

"When my father was president, everything here was full steam ahead. Everyone knew what they were doing and why. There was no stopping them. They knew they were building a company that provided a real service for our community. And the agency had a family feeling—it was about making a difference, having fun, and creating opportunities for everyone. My dad had an amazing effect on people. Being around him made everyone feel that what they were doing was important. There was real joy in the agency then. I've been trying to re-create that feeling, but it's not the same. Times have changed, and what worked for Dad doesn't necessarily work today."

Jim had said everything was "full steam ahead"—the phrase had caught my attention. "What exactly do you mean by 'full steam ahead'?" I asked.

"Well, that was a term used during the day of the steamships. It meant they were fully powered and moving ahead full force."

"Wasn't it also a phrase used in a war? I remember, 'Damn the torpedoes. Full steam ahead,'" I continued.

Jim smiled. "Now you've hooked me. I'm a bit of a history buff. That was Admiral Farragut in the Civil War. It might have been 'full steam ahead' or 'full speed ahead,' but you're right. He did say 'damn the torpedoes,' refusing to consider retreat in spite of the mines ahead. Why do you ask?"

"I was wondering if *full steam ahead* also means being reckless and blindly moving ahead in the face of danger."

"No, I think it's the opposite. It means having vision—being so clear about your purpose, so committed to it, and so sure about your ability to accomplish it, that you move ahead decisively despite any obstacles."

Jim paused a second and added, "That's exactly what my father was like."

"He sounds pretty special. I bet you miss him."

"I sure do."

We sat in silence a few moments.

"Jim, would you tell me more about what your father did here?" I asked, thinking it would help me get to know Jim better.

"That's easy." He paused and then said, "Dad had a vision of what this place was going to be. And everyone else here shared it. The most amazing thing about this place was the tremendous amount of energy, excitement, and passion. Everyone really believed in the vision and what they were doing. They felt they were going to make a difference. They wanted to change the way insurance agencies were viewed. And they did, for our agency. They built a strong reputation for excellent services and grew rapidly. They had to move into a bigger building within the first three years, and then again five years later. Everyone in the agency knew what they were doing and why. And even though they weren't all close friends, there was a strong sense of trust and respect. Managers didn't try to control. They let others assume responsibility because they knew everyone shared the vision and were clear about their goals and direction.

People had the power to make some pretty important decisions. They didn't have to run everything by my father and other top managers. Everyone assumed responsibility for their own actions. They took charge of their future, not passively waiting for it to happen. There was a lot of room for creativity. People could make their contributions in their own way, and those differences were respected because everyone knew they were in the same boat together, all part of a larger whole."

"Going full steam ahead!" I added.

Jim laughed. "Well, yes, that's exactly it."

"It sounds powerful," I mused.

"It's the power of a shared vision," Jim replied. "I know, because I've experienced it."

"So, we're back to the vision thing. What does it mean to have a vision?" I wondered.

"I think when you have a vision you are fully powered, knowing where you're going, and moving ahead full force."

"So, *full steam ahead* really does describe the power of vision!"

Jim smiled and then grew serious. "The problem is times have changed. We're bigger, the industry has changed, it's more complicated with legislation and red tape, and there are so many new people here who didn't know Dad or grow up in the industry. Maybe our vision needs to be renewed or expanded to include all that has changed. I have a lot of sympathy for former president George H. Bush when he struggled trying to understand the 'vision thing.' Sometimes I tell myself it's really not important to have a vision— all we need is a well-run, operationally solid, financially sound company. But then I remember how it used to be. And I know that something important is missing. I've worked hard to be a good manager, but it's not enough. Leadership is about going somewhere."

I was amazed and honored that he was sharing such deep concerns with me. I really wasn't sure how to respond except to return the same kind of honesty he was giving me.

"Jim, I love the warm atmosphere here and felt welcome and comfortable right away. But I think you're right about the importance of vision. It seems to me that if your vision isn't clear to you, it can't really be clear for all of us who work here. If you could get clear on where you want to take the agency, maybe the shift you're hoping for would occur."

I paused a moment and continued.

"So, if you don't have a vision, how do you get one? What is it that makes a vision?" I wondered.

Jim startled me by laughing. "You ask a lot of questions, Ellie."

"I know," I replied sheepishly, suddenly embarrassed. "It's gotten me into trouble before."

"Well, I like it," Jim responded kindly. "I like your candor and your fresh perspective. You don't take anything for granted. You make me think."

Jim then made an offer that changed my life. "Ellie, if you're interested, I'd like to talk with you some more and figure out what this 'vision thing' is all about together."

Without a moment's hesitation, I replied, "Where do we start?"

"I think we should start by taking this 'vision thing' apart and understanding what makes a vision compelling—something that people really want to be part of and that provides direction."

"And when do we start?"

Jim replied, "I come in early almost every morning. I like to sit here quietly before the rush of the day begins. It's a great time for thinking and reflection. No one's discovered my secret hideout until now. How about using this time to think about vision?"

"Sounds good to me. Same time, same place tomorrow."

• • •

Full steam ahead intrigued me. That night I did some research to see what I could find out about steam engines. I learned that the steam engine was without doubt one of the most influential inventions in the development of industry and civilization. In fact, the development of the steam engine made modern industry possible. Until then, people had to rely on their own muscles, the wind, or animals such as horses for power. One steam engine could do the work of hundreds of horses. It could supply all the power needed to run the machines in a factory. A steam locomotive could haul thousands of tons of freight. Steamships provided fast, dependable transportation. *Full steam ahead* certainly did describe the transformative power unleashed by vision!

I couldn't wait to share my discovery with Jim in the morning.

Element 1:
Significant Purpose

"That's great, Ellie," Jim congratulated me when I told him what I had learned. "The advent of the steam engine introduced a strong source of energy and power and created a transformation. Equating the power of vision with the power of the steam engine makes sense."

Jim continued. "Now I've got something to share with you. Remember when you pressed me to say what *full steam ahead* really means?"

"Yes. You said it means being fully powered, knowing where you're going, and moving ahead full force."

"That's right. I also said it means being so clear about your purpose, so committed to it, and so sure about your ability to accomplish it that you move ahead decisively despite any obstacles. Remember?"

"I remember," I smiled.

"Well, I woke up with an 'ah-ha.' I realized that *purpose* is one of the elements of a compelling vision. My father used to talk about *purpose* a lot. In fact, he was passionate about it. And he made sure everyone in the agency understood the purpose and supported it.

I think it was one of the secrets to Dad's vision."

I must have had a blank look on my face because he smiled at me and continued.

"By *purpose*, I mean understanding what we are here for, why we exist. It means understanding what business we are *really* in so that we all can focus our efforts in support of that purpose."

"I'm waking up a little slowly this morning," I replied. "But I think I'm with you."

"OK. What business do you think we are *really* in, Ellie?"

"That's easy," I replied. "The insurance business."

Jim paused a moment and said, "No, those are our products and services. But why do people purchase those products and services? What do they really want from us?"

I had to think about that a moment. I couldn't see where he was going with this. So, Jim took another approach. He said, "Ellie, have you made any purchases lately?"

"Hardly," I laughed. "No money. Oh, wait. I did splurge and buy a new mattress right after my husband left. But what's that got to do with anything?"

"Why did you buy it?"

I paused and reflected. I was a little embarrassed. It had been a spur-of-the- moment purchase—something I really didn't need and certainly couldn't afford. Maybe I was trying to clean out the last traces of Doug by getting rid of the bed we had shared, the way he had betrayed me and all. But I wasn't going to say any of that to Jim.

I thought about it for a moment. Why had I bought the particular mattress I did? What was I looking for in a mattress? Actually I had spent a great deal of time testing several different mattresses in the store. I had tried a variety of sleeping positions. I hadn't been sleeping well, partly because I was upset. But also our old mattress sagged slightly in the middle, and without Doug's body next to mine, I just sank into the sag. I was waking with a backache almost every morning. So, I was looking for a firm mattress that would hold its shape over the years and that would allow me to get a good night's rest. Then it occurred to me!

"I wanted to buy a good night's rest!" I blurted out.

Jim smiled. "So, that's the business they are *really* in. Now, what business are we *really* in here?"

I thought again. Why do people buy insurance? I had health insurance and car insurance. What did I really want when I purchased those policies?

"I think I get it! People who buy insurance want peace of mind for the future. They want financial security for possible worst-case scenarios such as serious illnesses, accidents, or death."

Jim grinned. "That's what I think, too! They want peace of mind for the future that doesn't diminish their peace of mind in the present by costing more than they can afford. And they want peace of mind in knowing they'll get the help they need if they need to place a claim.

"Our agents know what kind of questions to ask to find out exactly what peace of mind and security mean to each of our customers. That way they can help our customers choose the best products and services to fit their individual needs. And our customer service reps know that they need to support that sense of security when our customers have claims issues, need answers to questions about benefits, or need comparative pricing.

"Understanding what business we're really in is essential for everyone in our agency. It affects what products and services we provide, how we market them, and even how our receptionist answers the phone.

"My father believed, and so do I, that's a huge part of our success as a company. Our customers trust us because we know what business we're in from our customers' point of view. And we consistently act from that viewpoint."

I looked at him. "That's really powerful. So, you think purpose is an important part of a vision?"

"I do," Jim replied. "I think it's a key element."

"What about mission?" I asked. "I see all these statements on walls in places like the supermarket, the fast-food restaurant; actually, I think I saw one on the wall in the dry cleaners. Some have titles like 'Our Mission.' Is that the same as purpose?"

"Sometimes," Jim replied. "Good mission statements include a clear statement of purpose. Unfortunately, the term *mission* is so overused and has so many different meanings that it's become confusing.

I find it simpler to use the term *purpose*. But I don't think it matters what you call it as long as it explains 'Why do we exist?' and 'What business are we really in?'"

• • •

Later that morning I listened to Jim's morning voice-mail message. I wasn't at all surprised by what I heard.

Good morning, everyone. This is Jim. I want to congratulate everyone on our outstanding first quarter.

One of the ways we continue to pull off this team effort is by remembering what business we're really in. We provide insurance products. But this isn't what our customers really want. No one would voluntarily spend their money on insurance unless they could look in a crystal ball and know for sure they'd need it. But they do want to spend their money on peace of mind—peace of mind for the future without diminishing their peace of mind in the present.

We need to be sure that they are offered a package that meets their particular needs, within their own budget. How do we support our purpose, creating peace of mind? It might seem easier for those of you who have direct contact with our customers. But I challenge each of us to find how we support that purpose in our own way, no matter what our role is here in the agency. Remember why we exist—

what business we're in from our customers' point of view. Stay focused on our purpose, and we'll be able to keep up the good work! Have a great weekend, everyone!

By now I had gotten into the habit of transcribing Jim's messages each day. I wasn't exactly sure why I was still doing it, but it felt like the right thing to do. Besides, I could then read the messages and reflect further on this interesting new company and the intriguing man I was getting to know.

• • •

Over the weekend I thought about purpose. It was amazing that once I started looking, I began seeing it everywhere. "PURPOSE."

I watched the news at 7:00 Friday night and realized that a purpose of the major network news is to provide entertainment. The attractive news anchors, weather reporter, and sportscaster chatted easily with each other. They all seemed like friends and engaged in humor-filled banter. They offered an enjoyable way to catch up on the news.

My curiosity piqued, I switched to CNN. What a contrast! CNN clearly had a very different purpose. This wasn't about friendly entertainment. It was totally focused on the information—not the personalities. I wanted to learn more about CNN's purpose, so I went to its Web site and learned that it provides 24-hour coverage of in-depth, live and breaking national and global news as it unfolds. CNN focuses on different customers than the major networks do.

CNN's viewers are typically busy people who can't always schedule the time to sit in front of the television at 7:00 P.M. From their customers' viewpoint, CNN's purpose is to provide news-on-demand. CNN and the major network news have two very different purposes for two very different types of customer needs.

I then began an Internet search that took me through the weekend. I searched for both "purpose statements" and "mission statements." I spent hours looking at them.

Many of the statements were inspiring and focusing statements that explained why the company existed and what need it served from the customers' viewpoint. Others sounded so bland that I couldn't imagine they would inspire anyone. Some might be inspiring but were so general I couldn't imagine they would provide any focus or direction. One such statement was "Our mission is to walk our talk."

In the humor section, I found a "mission statement creator." You could create a mission statement by choosing from a list of nouns, verbs, adjectives, and adverbs. The statements it created sounded business-like to someone like me, using words like *empowerment*, *deliverables*, and *exceed expectations*. But they didn't mean anything and provided no clues as to what business you were in.

I came across several real mission statements that didn't sound a whole lot different from the humorous ones I had played with.

One well-known company's mission was "to exceed the expectations of our customers. We will accomplish this by committing to our shared values and achieving the highest levels of customer satisfaction." I wondered, *What business are they really in? What need do they fulfill from their customers' point of view? What purpose do they serve?*

It occurred to me that there are a lot of mission statements (my Internet search yielded over 3,700 matches), but there is not much agreement or consistency on what belongs in a mission statement.

Even most of the purpose statements I found didn't explain why the company existed or what business they were in from their customers' viewpoint, as Jim had explained.

Most purpose and mission statements merely described the products and services they provided at best and at worst were a meaningless collection of platitudes.

I did find a clear and inspiring mission statement from the Yarmouth Fire Department: "We will do our best to protect people and property in Yarmouth from harm, to improve their safety, to educate the public to prevent emergencies and provide quick and effective responses." I thought, *This is what I, from a customers' viewpoint, want from a fire department; they are thinking about their purpose from a results viewpoint, not just a service-provided viewpoint.* I hoped the firefighters in the city in which I lived saw their purpose in a similar manner.

In contrast, I read the mission statement of a police department from another city. It said that their purpose was "to enforce the law." I found myself asking, "To what end?" In other words, *why* did they provide that service—to "enforce the law"? I thought a better statement would be "to defend citizen's constitutional rights and protect people from harm." That would be a much more compelling and focusing purpose, in my opinion.

Still on the Internet, I found the mission statement for Merck, a pharmaceutical company. Its stated mission is "to provide society with superior products and services that preserve and improve the quality of life." Now, that's a noble purpose! Its products and services are pharmaceutical, but its *purpose*, the reason why it produces pharmaceuticals, is "to improve the quality of life." *What does Merck do to improve the quality of life?* I wondered. Searching the Web site further I discovered that the company did indeed support its purpose. One example is the Mectizan Donation Program. In 1987, Merck developed a drug that treats a third world disease known as "river blindness." Unfortunately, the people at risk for river blindness could not afford to purchase the medicine. Knowing they would not make a profit on this drug, Merck developed it anyway and has donated it ever since to more than thirty million people a year. *Can they have a noble purpose and do well financially?* I wondered. Merck's Web site featured the words of their founder George

W. Merck: "We try never to forget that medicine is for the people. It is not for the profits. The profits follow." Looking at the company's financial performance, it appears that the founder's guiding philosophy was correct as Merck continues to produce a competitive return year after year.

It was becoming obvious to me that a good purpose statement needed to explain "why" and it needed to "serve a greater good."

Later in the weekend, I did a search of newspaper and magazine articles. I found an interesting article in the *New York Times*. Harvey Mackay, chairman of Mackay Envelope Company in Minneapolis, had adopted the statement "to be in business forever." That didn't seem to meet the criteria of a good statement—it was fuzzy and not inspiring or focusing. But as I read on, I realized that the statement actually had meaning to the employees of Mackay Envelope. According to Mackay, "The emphasis on staying in business forever tells employees to focus on the long term and not to push too hard a bargain with customers and suppliers because customers might go to other companies and suppliers might give their best new technologies to competitors." This statement didn't clarify what business Mackay Envelope was in, but it did convey more meaning than I had originally thought.

I began to realize that the most important thing was the *meaning* of the statement—and not simply what it said. The best words in the world would be meaningless if they meant nothing to the people in the organization. I realized having a mission statement didn't necessarily create focus and inspiration. On the other hand, a good statement of purpose that really held meaning for the people in the company could have a lot of power.

• • •

I was absorbed all weekend by my investigations of purpose and mission, and I could hardly wait to discuss it with Jim. Monday, promptly at 6:30 A.M., I tested the back door of the office building and let myself in. Jim seemed to be waiting for me.

"Well?" he asked.

I told him all about my weekend search. I must have talked nonstop for fifteen minutes before I paused to take a deep breath. Then I said, "I think this sums it up." I handed him an piece of notepaper on which I had written:

PURPOSE

- Purpose is your organization's reason for existence.

- It answers the question "Why?" rather than just explaining what you do.

- It clarifies—from your customers' viewpoint—what business you are *really* in.

- Great organizations have a deep and noble sense of purpose—a *significant* purpose—that inspires excitement and commitment.

- The words themselves are not as important as their meaning to the people.

Jim studied the notepaper silently for a long time. I waited anxiously, wondering what he would think. Had I overstepped my bounds? Who was I to be presenting my views to the president of a successful company? I wasn't an MBA graduate. I hadn't even held my first real job for more than two weeks.

Although I was so engrossed in this project all week-end that I had hardly thought about Jim, I was now painfully aware of how much I wanted his approval. The longer he took to respond, the lower I slumped into my chair.

Jim finally looked up, his eyes resting on mine, and then he flashed a warm smile that made me melt. I didn't know what he was going to say, yet I knew that whatever he said, I would feel good about myself and about him. But what he said next actually startled me.

"That's great! You've summed up in five simple statements something it took me years to learn from my father. This confirms that we've made the right decision to work together to figure this out."

Jim taped my card on the wall near our table.

"This card will be the beginning of our road map!" he remarked.

We paused and looked at the card in silence.

"Did you find any answers to your question on the difference between mission and purpose?" he asked next.

I told him what I had found. "An effective mission statement includes clear purpose. Unfortunately, most don't."

I continued. "In order for a mission statement to be effective, it needs to include a statement of clear purpose as we've defined it. A good mission statement might also include a description of how the people in a company deliver on the purpose, what their products and services are, and how they support the purpose. However, a mission statement that only describes what they provide or how they provide it, without explaining purpose, is unfocused, unmotivating, and meaningless."

"Makes sense to me," Jim replied.

"Now I have a question for you," I continued.

"Uh-oh," Jim teased. "I'm learning to watch out for those innocent questions of yours."

"Really, I'm serious!" I waited for his attention. "I started asking you last week about the purpose of your morning voicemail messages. It seemed you weren't clear. You felt leaving them was important, but you didn't know why. Now that we've investigated purpose more, I'd like to ask you again. Why do you leave your voicemail messages?"

"OK, Ellie. You're right. I don't know. But I'll come back to you with an answer. I'm leaving for an association conference later this morning and will be gone the rest of the week. I'll think about it while I'm gone. How's that?"

"Great!" I replied. "Have a good trip."

As he left the room, I continued to sit at the table staring after him. Gone for the rest of the week? I was struck by how much I would miss our morning time together and how important our friendship was becoming to me. How long had it been since I had felt that kind of comfort in the presence of a man? When did Doug and I stop feeling comfortable together? I began to realize that Doug and I had left each other long before he got involved in his affair. I suddenly felt so sad. I just sat there and cried, and was really glad no one was around.

. . .

I spent the rest of the week applying what I had learned about purpose to my own job. I wanted to learn what everyone's responsibilities were—not just my own. I must have been a pest, asking as many questions as I did. But no one seemed to mind. In fact, they seemed to appreciate the fact that I was genuinely interested in what they were doing. If I were ever to understand the *purpose* of tax accounting, I needed to understand the *business* of tax accounting.

As far as I could tell, we were responsible for preparing quarterly and year-end tax returns. To do this, we needed to collect information from people who often indicated they were too busy and had other priorities. All in all, it didn't sound like a very exciting purpose. The people who worked in this part of the accounting department were very nice, but you could hardly call them inspired. And I didn't have a clue about how any of this helped create peace of mind for our customers.

I took out my list and reviewed it. I thought about the third point—*Purpose explains what business you're in from your customers' viewpoint*—and realized that I hadn't gotten our customers' viewpoint.

I had to think a moment about who our customers were. It was so easy to assume that senior management or the government was our customer. But that didn't seem to fit with what Jim had been saying. I thought about the people who supplied tax-related information—the agents, customer service reps who track claims, and even some people in the accounting department. They were always so busy, and sometimes I didn't get all the information I needed right away. Were they my customers, or was I their customer?

During breaks and lunch, I started informal conversations with several of these people and asked them what they thought. Was there a way that tax accounting served them? Was there a need that we fulfilled? What service or value did they believe we provided (or could provide) for their work and for the agency? Was there a way that they were our customers?

Although most people I questioned seemed genuinely willing to take the time to talk, they weren't quite sure how to respond. No one had ever asked them these kinds of questions before. I got the impression that people from the tax accounting department often acted like the "tax police," requesting data, making sure it was correct and on time.

After several discussions over the next couple of days, I surmised that these people really were our customers because we could help them and the agency by

- helping increase our agency's profitability by finding ways to reduce the overall tax burden;
- helping ensure compliance (that we were being honest and ethical in our reporting to the government);
- providing tax advice to help them make effective business decisions.

I shared what I had learned with Marsha, who was both surprised and interested. "That's a different way of looking at tax accounting," she remarked.

Marsha started thinking out loud.

"We need to be business partners with our customers by supplying the information they need and finding ways to minimize the agency's tax burden.

"This means we shouldn't just be collecting data and completing forms. We need to be proactive in getting the right information to the right people.

"If we view our work this way, it will change the way we work with other departments. We'll stop thinking and acting like 'the tax police.' We'll become proactive, valued business partners if we can figure out how to do this right. I've always known our work was important. But now I think it might actually get to be fun."

She thought a moment further and continued enthusiastically. "This way of looking at our work would help not only tax accounting but the entire accounting department. So often we see ourselves, and are seen by others, as 'number crunchers' rather than business partners. I can already see that when we look at purpose from this viewpoint, one of the purposes of the accounting department is to supply accurate and timely information to help our partners make good business decisions."

Marsha paused and considered. "I think we should have a department meeting to discuss this and agree on our purpose."

I smiled. "It feels so good to have my thoughts and opinions appreciated. It's part of what I love about working here."

"When I hear a good idea," Marsha said, "I like to act on it quickly. But that's not always true in other organizations. In fact, it's probably not the case in every department in our agency. But it's my style and the way I like to run our department."

"Works for me!" I laughed.

• • •

Throughout the week, I looked forward eagerly each morning to Jim's voicemail message, which he left on the system even when he traveled. As I listened to his messages, I felt I got to know him even better. Everything I learned about him made me like him more. I looked forward to his return so we could resume our morning investigations.

The three previous weeks had literally flown by, and I had hardly seen my children, so I decided to spend the weekend reconnecting with them. But it seemed they had other ideas. Every time I suggested we do something, they had conflicting plans.

Alex hardly spoke to me at all. When he did, it was in monosyllables without consonants at the ends of words. Whenever I asked a question, he responded with a kind of grunt. I wondered whether something had happened to his vocal cords. I assumed that this was part of becoming a teenager. So I gave him a bit of space.

Jen didn't have much to say, either. I found a note from school about upcoming soccer practices. When I asked her about it, she said she wasn't going to participate in soccer this year. I was surprised because last year she had enjoyed it so much. But when I tried to discuss it with her, she just shrugged.

So I spent much of the weekend fixing things up— shopping, doing laundry, and handling other things on which I had gotten behind. I drove the kids and their friends to the movies and to the mall. Monday morning I left for work with a well-stocked refrigerator, a clean house, and a strong desire to see Jim.

• • •

He was there—as I had hoped! The minute I saw him I realized how much I had missed him. He stood when I entered the room and smiled as he greeted me. "Ellie! You've been busy while I've been gone."

"How did you know?"

"Marsha left me a message about your upcoming department meeting this week. Seems like you've gotten her excited. That's pretty fast work for the new kid on the block!"

We both laughed, and I asked about his trip.

"It was wonderful. This association conference is something I look forward to every year." He continued casually, "At the end of the conference, we stayed in Colorado to ski with some of my closest friends and their wives."

Wives? My ears perked up, but I didn't react. My smile froze on my face. Maybe he meant his friends' wives. No one had mentioned anything about a wife. But then, why would they? No one even knew about my morning talks with Jim.

"So, how was the skiing?" I asked evenly.

"It was great! There's nothing like skiing in the Rockies."

Then he said it. Somehow I knew it was coming.

"Carolyn and I love to ski at Aspen. It's our favorite resort."

I said, "Aspen?" I really meant, *Carolyn?* I needed to think about this. I excused myself with a sudden headache and fled the room.

The office was empty when I went to my cubicle. It felt good to sit there alone. I needed to think this through. I was attracted to Jim and felt really special when I was with him. But he was married. I could never do to another woman what Diane had done to me. Still, it was important to me to continue to build a relationship with Jim.

I wondered how he felt about me. I know he really liked me, but now I wasn't sure exactly in what way. He had never put out any of those signals—the flirting kind of signals. He was just genuinely nice and interested in me as a person.

I wondered what else could there be? I felt I was headed into uncharted territory. I wanted a close, personal relationship—a *real* friendship. I didn't have a clue how to do it, and I wasn't sure what he wanted. It seemed too soon to discuss any of this with him, so I decided to continue as before, without defensiveness, but with clear boundaries. I felt disappointed yet, at the same time, relieved. In some ways a potential burden was removed. Now we were free to be ourselves without a big question looming overhead.

Later that morning, I thought some more about Jim. He seemed to be getting something from me, although I wasn't quite sure what. He clearly appreciated my questions. It was as though we were on a discovery journey together. Maybe I was helping him put his ideas into words. Perhaps I was helping him discover the principles behind his actions. And possibly, just possibly, we were uncovering some concepts that would help the agency move forward into the future.

Jim's morning message seemed to confirm my thoughts. He answered the question I had been asking him: why he was leaving these voicemail messages.

Good morning, everyone. This is Jim. I'd like to explain some of the reasons I've been leaving these messages.

The first one is that I want to remind people to stay in the present and enjoy life. And I want us to keep perspective—to remember to get our egos out of the way and not think that we're the centers of the universe. I guess that's been a constant theme.

Second, I want to help maintain our sense of community as we grow, so that we can harness our collective energy for the benefit of us all. And, I want to catch people doing things right and acknowledge their contributions. I think it's really great that so many of you send messages back to me. And I'm glad I've had an opportunity to forward so many of your views back to everyone.

Third, I want to share myself, my life as a person, what I am doing, what and who touches me, my struggles and joys, and what I'm learning.

Fourth, I want to remind us to stay focused on our purpose—what business we're really in. This is very important as we continue to grow. We need to remember why we exist.

Have a great day!

That day, as I transcribed Jim's message, I considered how I was influencing Jim. As a result of my questioning, he was becoming clear about the purpose of his morning messages, which would in turn allow him to be more focused in achieving that purpose. It reaffirmed that I really could add value in this growing relationship—if only by continuing to ask questions. I, too, was benefiting from our conversations. I could feel some measure of self-worth returning. It felt good to see my contributions making a difference.

Things were looking up at work. But they were not looking so great at home. This past weekend I had made an attempt to reconnect with my children, although they hadn't noticed it. At least I was resuming some of my neglected duties, such as shopping for food and cleaning the house. Reflecting on this, I decided to go to a PTA meeting at Jen's school that evening.

I had been active in the PTA in the past and I liked her school. The school administration encouraged parent involvement, and I had always felt welcome there, although I hadn't been very involved in the past year.

•••

The PTA meeting began with a presentation by the principal on the results of the recent standardized tests. Our school was slightly above average for our state, and he made a big deal about that (although our state was slightly below average for the country). There was a lot of discussion of test scores and what they actually meant. A variety of concerns were expressed, and people began to offer suggestions for improving the school. Someone suggested that the school should put more emphasis on writing skills next year. Someone else suggested expanding the math program.

In the midst of a heated discussion on the importance of math versus art, I raised my hand and asked simply, "Excuse me, but I'd like to ask a question that might help us answer some of these other questions." All heads turned toward me. I continued, "It could help me if someone could tell me the purpose of our school."

Dead silence.

The principal cleared his throat and said, "We have a mission statement."

"Could you tell me what it is?"

"It's framed and hanging in my office."

"Could you just tell me basically what it says?"

"Well, it's about providing a quality education for all our students. Highest standards. You know, that stuff."

Applying my new knowledge of the power of purpose, I asked, "To what end?"

No response.

I pressed on. "I mean, why are we providing a quality education for all our students? What is the purpose of educating children? We seem to be talking about the education business. What we need to be in is the *learning* business—and make sure that learning has occurred. We need to be really clear about what we mean by learning and what kind of learning we mean."

I couldn't believe I had blurted out all of that.

The PTA head added, "I think you're onto something, Ellie. Maybe before we jump into problem solving, we should take some time to reflect on what our school is about."

Several other parents agreed immediately, and the principal suggested, "Could we form a group of teachers and parents to work on this and report back at our next meeting?"

Everyone agreed and the principal then nominated me to co-chair the committee with him. Me and my big mouth!

So, there I sat, mentally kicking myself for speaking up, thinking that now I was in way over my head. But before I knew it, we had the names of eight committee members. And everyone was smiling at me as though I knew what I was doing.

• • •

I couldn't wait to see Jim the next morning. I arrived at 6:00 and actually got there before he did. I waited at the back door for him. He showed up at about 6:15.

He smiled a hello as he pressed the keys to unlock the door and deactivate the alarm.

"Is this the time you usually arrive?" I asked as I followed him into the building.

"Yes," he answered. "Carolyn usually walks early in the morning with some friends. And I like to get here to spend some quiet time alone before the hectic day begins." He smiled and continued, "At least I used to like to spend the time alone. Lately I've been enjoying spending the time in reflective conversation with my new friend."

He paused a moment and then continued, "I find myself looking forward to our morning conversations. I think I'm finally going to find the 'sparkle' at work that I've been hoping for. And, I'm enjoying getting to know you."

He then looked me steadily in the eye and said, "Ellie, I realized yesterday when I told you about Carolyn that I haven't talked about my family. Carolyn and I have been married over twenty-five years, and we have a daughter, Kristen, who is a senior in college. My family is a very important part of my life."

"Of course," I answered. "I hope to meet them someday."

I understood that Jim was defining our relationship. It was clear that we were destined to be more than just business colleagues, but there would be no romance. Maybe the best way to describe our developing relationship would simply be to call it "special." At that point, I totally let go of any fantasies I might have been harboring and was able to concentrate on the true possibilities.

Having more clarity on our relationship made it easier for me to ask Jim's help. I told him about the PTA meeting and how totally unprepared I felt to lead this committee. "I need some help—your help, to be specific."

"I certainly empathize with your situation," he offered. "But I think it's the principal's job to define the purpose. I think you should go back to the principal and tell him he should just do it and that a committee isn't needed."

"You mean he should just figure it out by himself and then tell everyone?" I asked. For some reason that didn't sit right with me. Our principal might be able to figure it out by himself, but he didn't have a charismatic personality. I couldn't see him explaining the school's purpose in a way that would inspire others and ensure their commitment. And if he did this alone, how could we be sure it would provide focus for these important decisions and not just end up being framed on a wall, forgotten forever?

"Jim, I just don't know. My gut tells me that the administration, teachers, parents, and maybe even the students need to be involved. I think the idea of a representative committee makes sense."

"OK," Jim responded. "Trust your instincts."

"The problem is the principal has asked me to put together the agenda for the meeting, and I'm not sure what to do. I've never chaired a meeting before."

Jim helped me plan for the meeting. We concluded that after the committee identified a clear purpose, it needed to be discussed at the next PTA meeting—and not just presented. By the time we were finished, we had a good agenda for the meeting and a game plan for moving forward. I felt much more confident. Jim was a great sounding board, and I was glad I had a partner to help me on this journey!

• • •

Wednesday morning as we chatted, Jim mentioned, "So, today's a big day for the accounting department."

"How's that?" I asked.

"Isn't this the day of your meeting to look at purpose?"

"You're right!" I had forgotten Marsha had called the meeting for first thing in the morning. *This will be interesting* I thought. *I'll get a chance to see how the power of purpose makes a difference.*

Jim's morning message set the tone for the day.

 Good morning, everyone. This is Jim. I'd like to tell you a story this morning that illustrates the power of understanding the purpose of your work. Three workers were busy constructing a building when an observer approached. The first worker was dirty, sweaty, and had an unhappy expression on his face.

The observer asked the first worker, "What are you doing?" The worker replied, "I'm laying bricks." The second worker also was dirty, sweaty, and had an unhappy expression on his face. The observer asked the second worker, "What are you doing?" The second worker replied, "I'm making $20 an hour." The third worker was dirty and sweaty but had a beautiful and inspired expression. He worked as hard as the other two, but work seemed to come more effortlessly for him. The observer asked the third worker, "What are you doing?" And he replied, "I'm building a cathedral." I encourage you to look at your work from the perspective of its purpose, not just the activities you are doing.

During the department meeting, Marsha asked me to share my list of criteria for purpose and what I had learned from our customers' viewpoint. Everyone was intrigued. There was a robust discussion. Based on our customers' perspective, we created a statement of purpose that explained what business we were in. We decided the next step would be to each test our statement with our various "customers" to see if it made sense and, also, to get their ideas on the best ways we could accomplish our purpose. We all left the meeting enthusiastic and focused. It was refreshing!

I walked out of the meeting impressed by how much the power of purpose had energized the group. The lively discussions had been an important part of creating that energy. If everyone had just been handed a typed document from Marsha, I doubt that it would have had much impact at all. The meeting reinforced my view that involving others besides the leader is important—and that it would be far better for the PTA committee to work on purpose as a team rather than charge the school principal to do it on his own.

But I had an uneasy feeling that something was missing. It seemed that, as important as purpose was, there had to be something else.

Element 2:
Clear Values

At the end of the week, Jim left on another short trip, this time to a college reunion. One morning, while listening to his morning voicemail message, I figured out what was missing, at least part of what was missing.

 Good morning, everyone. This is Jim. It's a little after 7:00. This ends a fabulous trip, surrounded by colleagues and old friends, people I have known for many years. It's been a time that nurtured my values.

I'd like to read you my values:

"I value spiritual peace. I know that I'm living by this value anytime I realize that God loves me no matter what I do, anytime I am grateful for my blessings, and anytime I pray and feel God's unconditional love."

I felt a lot of that here. I got up early every morning and entered my day slowly, and really got into a sense of being at peace.

Then my second value:

"I value joy. I know that I am living by this value anytime I am feeling playful and anytime I wake up feeling grateful for my blessings, the beauty around me, and the people in my life."

Being around old friends is really a joy. We've had a lot of fun. We've known each other before we were anything, and all of us have done quite well. But we all keep each other grounded here because none of us is overly impressed with our accomplishments.

And my third value: "I value health. I know I'm living by this value anytime I treat my body with love and respect."

Just being in the mountains makes it easy to be aware of eating right and exercising. I'm aware that I've gotten out of shape, and I've decided that I'm going to keep this up when I get back home.

That was what was missing! *Values!*

It was obvious that Jim was led by his values. He lived them on a daily basis. He was clear about his values.

Values! *What does that word really mean? Why are values important? How are they connected to purpose?* All day long these questions reverberated in the back of my mind.

That night I searched for the definition in Jen's dictionary.

Value: "the quality of a thing that makes it wanted or desirable; e.g., the value of true friendship."

Values: "beliefs or ideals."

That's not a very sophisticated definition, I thought.
Then again, values shouldn't be a sophisticated concept.
Yet, it seemed to me that values are more than just
beliefs—they are deeply held beliefs. People care pas-
sionately about their values. We all feel good when we
act on our values.

Using that information, I wrote this definition:

> *Values are deeply held beliefs that certain qualities*
> *are desirable. They define what is right or*
> *fundamentally important to each of us.*
> *They provide guidelines for our choices and actions.*

If purpose is important because it explains "why,"
then values are important because they explain "how."

They answer the question "How will you behave
on a day-by-day basis as you fulfill your purpose?"

That was it!

To test my theory, I went back to the Internet to
look at the companies that had a good mission or
purpose. Did they also have clear values?

I returned to Merck's Web site. Bingo! Right
below their mission, they listed their values—five of
them—and each was clearly defined:

• *Our business is preserving and improving human
life.* All of our actions must be measured by our success in achieving this goal. We value above all our
ability to serve everyone who can benefit from the
appropriate use of our products and services, thereby
providing lasting consumer satisfaction.

- *We are committed to the highest standards of ethics and integrity.* We are responsible to our customers, to Merck employees and their families, to the environments we inhabit, and to the societies we serve worldwide. In discharging our responsibilities, we do not take professional or ethical shortcuts. Our interactions with all segments of society must reflect the high standards we profess.

- *We are dedicated to the highest level of scientific excellence and commit our research to improving human and animal health and the quality of life.* We strive to identify the most critical needs of consumers and customers; we devote our resources to meeting those needs.

- *We expect profits, but only from work that satisfies customer needs and benefits humanity.* Our ability to meet our responsibilities depends on maintaining a financial position that invites investment in leading-edge research and that makes possible effective delivery of research results.

- *We recognize that the ability to excel—to most competitively meet society's and customers' needs—depends on the integrity, knowledge, imagination, skill, diversity, and teamwork of employees, and we value these qualities most highly.* To this end, we strive to create an environment of mutual respect, encouragement, and teamwork—a working environment that rewards commitment and performance and is responsive to the needs of employees and their families.

Merck's values were so easy to find, right on the first page of its Web site—not just framed and tacked to a wall somewhere. Clearly, its mission and values are crucial to its identity as a company.

Then I studied an article from the *New York Times.* "This is the glue that holds this corporation together," said Michael J. Carey, vice president of Johnson & Johnson. "The message is the ability to produce business results, not at any cost, but within our value system." The article described how their values guided them through one of its worst crises: the 1982 incident in which cyanide placed into a bottle of Tylenol killed a customer. The company quickly recalled the product at a cost of $75 million. They paid a tremendous short-term cost. However, the long-term benefit is that the company not only survived a major crisis but emerged even stronger.

I tried to imagine the discussion of the people who participated in that important decision. They didn't have a lot of time to make it. Did anyone suggest just recalling the bottles in the city where the customer died? Did anyone suggest withholding the information? Did anyone suggest trying to find a scapegoat and blame someone else?

The only way they could make a quick and right decision that day was to use their values to guide them. That difficult decision was in the long-term best interest of the company and the public.

I revisited the Web site for CNN. What interested me was that this organization used its values on the "employment opportunities" page to attract the kind of people who would fit its culture. I read, "We want employees who—above all—have a passion for delivering the news in fast, accurate, and compelling ways to the global public we serve. We are looking for CNN's future: people with fresh ideas, innovative viewpoints, a willingness to work hard, and a commitment to the highest standards of journalism." Five values jumped out: fast, accurate, innovative, hard work, and highest standards of journalism.

When reading these companies' values, I was struck by how important it is for a company to state its values clearly so that it can attract employees whose values are aligned with the company's.

• • •

I couldn't wait for Jim's return to share my discovery. The minute I saw him, I didn't even say hello. Instead I said, "Purpose tells *why*. Values tell *how*."

Jim laughed. "That's a strange way to greet a friend you haven't seen for a while!"

"No, really, it's true. I get it!"

Purpose tells why. Values tell how.

I excitedly told Jim all about my investigations and how I had discovered that the companies that had a significant purpose also had clearly articulated values.

I handed Jim an piece of notepaper on which I had written:

VALUES

- Values provide broad guidelines on how you should proceed as you pursue your purpose.

- They answer the questions "What do I want to live by?" and "How?"

- They need to be clearly described so you know exactly the behaviors that demonstrate that the value is being lived.

- They need to be consistently acted on, or they are only "good intentions."

- People's personal values need to be in line with the values of the organization.

Jim studied the notepaper. "You're right! Values must be another key element of vision." He then taped my notepaper on the wall next to the other card titled "Purpose." Our road map was developing.

"What are the values here—for the agency?"

Jim mused, "That's a good question, Ellie. I think they were simply understood when we were a smaller company and my father was president. We've never articulated them."

"The best companies have values that support their purpose," I said. "Or so it seemed when I did my Internet search."

"That makes sense because values guide people's behavior and decisions on a daily basis as they pursue that purpose. When I think of the understood but not articulated values that are in place at our agency, I immediately think of 'ethics' and 'relationships.'"

"How do those values help fulfill the purpose of the agency?" I wondered.

"We're in a business that builds peace of mind. This means people need to trust us. They can't trust us unless we act ethically and develop positive relationships."

"Of course," I remarked. "And it means we need to treat each other according to these values also, doesn't it?"

"Absolutely. The values that guide our behaviors with our customers should guide how we behave with each other within the agency."

Jim continued, "I think there's one more value that's important for us—success. If we don't deliver on our promises, we won't grow our business."

"Makes sense to me," I remarked. "Do others in the agency agree?"

"Time to find out!" Jim smiled, stood up, and excused himself.

•••

Later that morning, I was not at all surprised to hear the following voicemail message:

 Good morning, everyone. This is Jim. Last week I talked about my personal values. Today I'd like to talk about another way of looking at values. Organizations also have values—understood norms that guide our behaviors on a daily basis. I've been thinking about what values should be guiding us here, and I'd like to test them out. I believe we need values around ethics, relationships, and success, and we need to identify behaviors that demonstrate what these values look like. We need to be sure we're all acting consistently with our values, and we need to help each other do that. So, I'd like to start talking about this. Do you agree that these are our values, and if so, how do we demonstrate them?

Jim's message reinforced for me how important it is to describe values in terms of examples of specific behaviors that support them. When Jim shared his personal values, he didn't just say that he valued health. He explained what it looks like when he is acting on that value and what he intends to do to support that value. Now, he was inviting people in the agency to help identify what it looks like when they are acting on the company's values.

• • •

The next morning, as we sat comfortably drinking our coffee, I remarked, "Your voicemail message yesterday seemed to have energized things. Everyone at lunch was talking about the agency's values."

"Great. This is a long overdue conversation. I've gotten a lot of replies on my voicemail already. I'm going to push to make them as clear as the examples you found on the Internet!"

"You know, Jim, this values stuff is really important. I see how the best companies are clear about their values and use them to guide behaviors and decisions. But why do you think it's so important?"

"I've been thinking about that, too," Jim responded. "Being clear about my personal values has been powerful for me. There's a lot of power in values. I think it's because values tap into people's feelings. People cherish their values and are deeply emotional about them. When they act in support of their values, they are proud of their actions."

"So we might say that values serve as the driving force behind purpose. Values supply the energy and excitement that help people remain committed when the going gets tough," I replied.

"Yes, when personal values are consistent with those of the organization, there's more commitment and greater pride in the organization. The overall quality of work improves. You might say that one reason clearly stated values are important is that they help ensure emotional commitment."

I considered this for a moment. "There could be a second reason. I think they also are unifying. Shared values help ensure consistency in how people throughout the organization behave. We had a lawn service back when I could afford things like that. Doug had hired a company to fertilize our grass and kill the weeds. They came regularly in the summer. I had asked them to call ahead to let me know they were coming so I could pick up the kids' toys from the yard and make arrangements to take them somewhere else to play. It was unpredictable. Depending on who was doing the work, some would call ahead and some wouldn't. Some would even start spraying with toys scattered in the grass. It seemed like there were no consistent standards for environmental safety, yet that's an important value that if articulated would have guided every person who sprayed our lawn. Not only would they have consistently called first, they might even have picked up toys from the lawn if they came and I wasn't home."

Jim agreed. He considered further, "The values of a company depend on what business it is in. CNN values speed because its business is reporting late-breaking news. We value relationships because we help our customers create peace of mind. Values help shape a culture that will support the company's purpose. They're not just soft, 'nice-to-haves.' They're vitally important because they guide people as they pursue their purpose."

"Do you think it matters what order the values are listed in?" I asked.

I told Jim about the newspaper article I had found when investigating the organization's values that described how Johnson & Johnson's leaders used their values to make the right decisions during the Tylenol tampering crisis in the 1980s. "Their values, which they call their 'Credo,' are listed in order. Their number one value is to ensure quality, affordable products to the people who use their products. Their *last* value is making a sound profit for the business and a fair return to their stockholders.

"The article said that the way the leaders made that decision so quickly was to consult their values. It has occurred to me that if their values hadn't been listed in order, they might have made their decision based on their value of profitability, rather than concern for the well-being of their customers."

Jim considered what I was saying. "I think you're right. Kristen's last year in high school we took a family trip to Disney World. While there, I learned that safety is their number one value, and courtesy is their number two value. Ideally, they would act on all their values all the time. But if there was a conflict between values, they'd know which one to act on."

"So if a 'cast member' (employee) was answering a guest's question in a courteous way and a scream was heard, that cast member would immediately excuse himself and head toward the scream because his number one value just called."

Jim laughed. "Well, that would be a specific example."

"So, we've agreed that it's important to list your values in order of importance."

Jim agreed.

We sat quietly for a while, drinking our coffee and enjoying each other's company.

It was time to head off to work. Jim reflected, "We've uncovered a lot this morning. We've identified why it's important for organizations to articulate their values, and we've determined that it is important to list those values in the order of importance."

He then gave me one of his piercing blue-eyed smiles and said, "Well, Ellie. This means your PTA committee will need to look at purpose and values. Sounds like you've got your work cut out for you if you want to be able to go full steam ahead."

"Yikes! I almost forgot the meeting is tonight!"

• • •

The committee meeting went better than I had expected. I shared what Jim and I had discovered about the power of significant purpose and clear values. A lively discussion ensued. It ended up being a long meeting, but by the end, we had agreed on a significant purpose from the viewpoint of what business we were really in: promoting learning—teaching being an activity that supported that purpose, but not the purpose itself. And we identified the most important values.

We came up with the following statement: *to support the development of the whole person—for our young
children to learn how to learn, to love to learn, to develop
positive self-regard and respectful relationships with others.*

Our purpose: *to support the development of the whole
person.*

Our values: *learning, positive self-regard*, and *respectful relationships.*

This statement meant we wanted our children to
get a well-rounded education in *all* areas, some of
which might not be reflected in standardized test
scores.

The committee decided we needed to bring our
thinking to the next PTA meeting. The principal said
he felt certain that if the teachers, administrators, and
parents could agree on this purpose and values, the
tough program decisions would be much easier. He
was totally committed to moving forward and eager
to provide the leadership. I felt great!

• • •

The next few weeks rolled by. I was aware that when I
was at work, I had energy; and when I was home, I felt
exhausted. On weekends when the children were with
me, I went through the motions of driving them to
activities, preparing meals, and doing laundry. Other
weekends I watched a lot of TV. Either way, I had no
social life. Sunday nights I would perk up in anticipa-
tion of seeing Jim the next morning.

Jim wasn't always in the building by 6:30 A.M. One morning I waited for him in the rain for thirty minutes. He showed up at 7:00 and found me huddled under the awning, quite bedraggled. The next day he gave me a key to the building and showed me how to turn off the alarm system. After that, we adopted a pattern around our morning conversation time. When Jim wasn't going to come in early, he'd let me know the day before. He didn't expect me to show up, but he always seemed pleased when I did. And honestly, I usually did show up because our early morning conversations meant so much to me.

Element 3:
Picture of the Future

"There's still a missing piece to this 'vision thing'! It's not all there yet." Jim mused.

I agreed.

"OK, let's look at what we know so far. Purpose explains why you exist, right? And values explain how you act as you pursue your purpose. And we know that significant purpose and clear values energize and mobilize people. But here's the problem: Purpose and values alone don't explain where you're going. Vision is about going somewhere. There needs to be a sense of destination or direction."

"How about the Apollo Moon Project? Some people use it as an example of a vision."

"You mean to put a man on the moon by the end of the 1960s?"

"Yes. Alex is studying this in school right now. He told me that when John F. Kennedy initiated that project, the technology to achieve it did not even exist! NASA overcame what seemed like insurmountable obstacles to achieve that spectacular result."

"I bet there isn't a person who was alive at that time who doesn't remember what he or she was doing the day of the first moon landing," Jim remarked. "I think what makes it powerful is the picture. It's a clear picture of the future that you can imagine happening."

"That's it!" Jim exclaimed. "That's what's missing— 'a picture of the future'!

"Here's another example of the power of creating a picture," he continued excitedly. "Do you remember what happened in the 1976 Olympics?"

"Well, I was pretty young at the time," I admitted. "Tell me about it."

"I was particularly interested in the Olympics that year because a good friend of mine was competing. But he never had a chance because the Soviet athletes walked away with almost all the gold medals. They won more gold than any other country, even in events they weren't expected to win. Everyone was absolutely stunned. Some people questioned whether the athletes had been on some kind of drugs. But that wasn't the case. The key to their success was that their sports training had involved a technique called 'mental rehearsal,' where the athletes visualized their performance during the competition. Today this technique is commonly used in sports training. At that time, it was very new, and the results were remarkable.

"My daughter Kristen said that she used the technique of visualizing when she was learning to ski moguls—the bumpy hills on a steep slope. She told me that she had taken several lessons on how to ski the 'bumps' but still didn't have much confidence and felt awkward. One day as she stood at the top of a particularly bumpy run, she watched one of the skiers go down quite gracefully. In fact, it looked as if the skier were dancing, there was such grace and rhythm. Kristen then imagined herself skiing with the same kind of rhythm. She actually saw it in her mind. Guess what happened next? She did it. She 'danced' down the slope. Since then, Kristen has used visualization techniques in a variety of situations. She told me that many sports trainers have gone beyond the technique of mental rehearsal to focusing on visualizing the end result. In other words, instead of having the athletes mentally practice the gymnastics routine, the dives, or the ski run, they visualize themselves standing on the podium receiving the gold medal. Think of that!"

A picture of the end result!

I recalled that when I had investigated purpose and values, I had found a statement by CNN that its vision was to be "viewed by every nation on the planet, in English, and in the language of that region." This certainly was a clear picture of the end result—it was a picture of something happening in the future. When I closed my eyes, I could actually see it. Like Steve Jobs's vision of a computer on every desk. It was a crisp picture, not some vague concept such as to be "Number One" or "The Provider of Choice." Those statements provided no clarity on destination or direction.

We agreed that the third key element of a compelling vision is a picture of the future.

A picture of the future is a key element of vision.

This conversation reminded me of the weight I had gained after I had Jen. A year later, I was still twenty pounds overweight. The doctor put me on a diet, which I grudgingly followed. For weeks, I ate mouse-sized rations and felt deprived as I chomped on celery watching the rest of my family eat ice cream for dessert. I finally gave up. I decided that I'd rather be fat and happy than starving and miserable—except I wasn't really happy with the way I looked. So I was stuck.

That "stuck feeling" lasted for a few weeks, and then I found something that actually worked. I pulled my favorite blue jeans out of the drawer, the ones that didn't fit anymore, and hung them up in my bedroom. Each evening before I went to sleep I looked at them and imagined myself wearing them. I visualized how I would look in them. The next morning, I'd do the same thing. It was energizing and encouraging. I started the diet again, but this time with my energy focused on the picture of how I wanted to look, not on the ice cream I was missing out on. It made a huge difference! And I lost the weight.

Instead of focusing on what I was giving up, I had focused on the picture of what I wanted to create—to look good in my blue jeans.

I told this story to Jim. We agreed that we had
uncovered an important principle:

⟶ **The power of picture works when you focus
on what you want to create, not what you
want to get rid of.**

We need to be *proactive*, not *reactive*.

I left work that evening intrigued by the power of
picture. I have always been deeply moved by the vision articulated by Martin Luther King Jr. I had a
copy of his "I Have a Dream" speech at home. I got it
out, read it, and was struck by the powerful pictures
he created.

> I have a dream that one day on the red hills of
> Georgia *the sons of former slaves and the sons of for-*
> *mer slave owners will be able to sit down together* at
> the table of brotherhood. . . . I have a dream that
> *my four little children will one day live in a nation*
> *where they will not be judged by the color of their skin*
> but by the content of their character. . . . I have a
> dream that one day the state of Alabama . . . will be
> transformed into a situation where *little black boys*
> *and girls will be able to join hands with little white boys*
> *and girls and walk together as sisters and brothers.* . . .
> We will be able to speed up the day when all of
> God's children, black men and white men, Jews
> and Gentiles, Protestants and Catholics, will be
> able to *join hands and sing* in the words of that old

Negro Spiritual, Free at last! Free at Last! Thank God almighty, we are free at last!

These certainly were vivid pictures—if you closed your eyes, you could actually see them happening. They weren't vague statements about the importance of freedom and brotherhood, but clear pictures that demonstrate what it looks like. I concluded that there was a tremendous amount of power in having a clear picture of the desired end result.

Another thing that struck me about Dr. King's pictures was that they were pictures *only* of the end result, not the process of achieving it. He had left it up to us to figure out how to achieve the end result. But the pictures he created are enduring and continue to serve as a beacon.

The next morning I handed Jim a copy of Dr. King's speech and told him about the second under-lying principle I had uncovered.

➤ **The power of picture works when you focus on the end result, not the process to achieve it.**

We summarized on a notepaper what we had un-covered about the third element and then taped it on the wall next to the other elements:

PICTURE OF THE FUTURE

- A picture of the end result, something you can actually see, not vague

- Focus on what you want to create, not what you want to get rid of.

- Focus on the end result, not the process for getting there.

"When I read Dr. King's speech," Jim remarked, "I am struck that it does more than just create a picture of the end result. It also reveals underlying values such as brotherhood, unity, and mutual respect."

We'd finally uncovered them!

The three key elements of a compelling vision:
Significant Purpose
Clear Values
A Picture of the Future

We were feeling pretty pleased with ourselves as we sat back and reflected on what we had learned.

"Would it be a compelling vision if it didn't have all three elements?" I wondered.

"I don't think so. In the example of the Apollo Moon Project, NASA certainly had a clear picture of the end result, even though the process to achieve it was not clear. The picture focused NASA's energy, and its people accomplished amazing results—all because of the Picture of the Future. But since that time, they have never re-created that energy or momentum. The power ended."

"True," I remarked. "I would have thought they would have landed on Mars by now."

"I think it's because the underlying purpose was never clearly agreed on. Why were we doing it? Were we doing it to win the space race, to begin the Star Wars space defense initiative, or in the spirit of *Star Trek* 'to boldly go where no one has gone before'? And because there was no Significant Purpose, there was nothing to guide future decisions. NASA has shown neither clear direction nor outstanding performance since."

I considered those thoughts for a moment. "So that means that the Apollo Moon Project was not a vision— it was a goal, a goal with a powerful picture."

"Exactly," Jim agreed. "I think a vision is enduring. It continues to provide guidance as goals are achieved. One way to tell the difference between a goal and a vision is to ask, 'What next?' A vision offers clear direction for future activity and guides the setting of new goals once the current ones have been achieved. Without a vision, once the goal has been achieved, it's all over."

"That's a good way to put it," I said. "Do you think it applies in every situation?"

"Yes, I do. Take your example about losing weight. You had an image of the end result, but once you had achieved your desired weight, your goal was finished. Right?"

I thought about what he was saying. I did think he was right. Looking thin was only a goal, not a vision, even though I had a picture of the end result in my mind. Losing weight could be a step toward achieving something greater, such as a healthy body or a positive self-image, if I had been clear about that.

"I think we should come up with a crisp definition of a vision," I suggested. "If we do that, it will help you as you think of your vision for the company, and it will help me as I work with the accounting department and also with Jen's school."

This is what we decided:

VISION DEFINED

- Vision is knowing who you are, where you're going, and what will guide your journey.

"This definition really works!" Jim said. "It's a crisp definition, but much richer than any I've come across. It shows that all three elements are part of a vision. 'Knowing who you are' means being clear about your purpose. 'Where you're going' is the picture of the future. And, 'what will guide your journey' are your values."

"Totally," I agreed. "If you don't know who you are, it really doesn't matter where you're going."

"And if you're going somewhere, you need to be clear about the values that will guide your journey, to help you make the tough decisions when you hit obstacles," Jim added.

"It's what allows you to go 'full steam ahead,'" I said. "If you're on a powerful steamship, you can't control the weather. You know your final destination, but you might need to shift course a bit to ride out a bad storm or avoid an iceberg. Your values allow you to shift course in a way that keeps you in sight of your true destination."

"How do you know if your vision is really a compelling vision?" Jim wondered.

We created a checklist to use as a test to make sure that when you do identify your vision, it is indeed a compelling vision. Here's what we came up with:

TESTS OF A COMPELLING VISION

- Helps us understand what business we're *really* in

- Provides guidelines that help us make daily decisions

- Provides a picture of the desired future that we can actually see

- Is enduring

- Is about being "great"—not solely about beating the competition

- Is inspiring—not expressed solely in numbers

- Touches the hearts and spirits of everyone

- Helps each person see how he or she can contribute

We decided that if a vision could pass this test, there was a pretty good chance it would provide clear direction and would mobilize people.

We were both quite excited. We believed we were exploring and learning about something really important and powerful. Jim said that it was also fun—working on the pieces of this puzzle together. Together, we were figuring out things that neither of us would have done on our own. We agreed that we brought out the best in each other.

"Now," Jim announced thoughtfully, "the real challenge is to create a vision for the agency that passes this test."

• • •

The next morning, Jim's voice mail message reminded me that the importance of creating a vision is not just for organizations but also for us as individuals.

Good morning, everyone. This is Jim.

Last night I was working on something and thinking that we really have a choice, that good leadership and how we are in the world starts on the inside. We have two choices.

1. Whose are we going to be?

2. Who are we going to be?

You might say it sounds like they're the same. No, the first question asks "whose are we going to be?" which means: Who is your audience? Who are you playing to? Who are you trying to gratify?

I've said before that if you think your self-worth is a function of your performance plus the opinion of others, then you're caught in a trap that leaves your self-esteem up for grabs every single day. But if you're playing to a higher audience or higher set of values, that's a different thing. Now you can do what is right because you know it's the right thing to do, instead of being driven by other people's opinions of you. It's what allows you to act with integrity.

The second question has to do with who you are. What is your purpose? Why are you here? I think it's really important that we all think about why are we here and what are we trying to do. If you don't have a clear purpose, then you can be jerked around and taken in all kinds of directions because you don't really know why you're here.

If you can answer these questions and then can create some pictures in your mind of what it looks like when you are acting from that knowledge, you will be available to the joys and richness of living your life fully, moving full steam ahead.

Jim's message reminded me that the concepts we had discovered for creating a compelling vision were the same both for organizations and for individuals. Collectively and individually, we need a significant purpose, clear values, and a picture that shows us what these look like when we are living them consistently. It gives meaning to our lives and provides direction. It helps us get focused, get energized and get great results.

Blurry Vision

I had been working at the agency for over two months, and I was feeling pretty good. I liked work—the sense of accomplishment it gave me. I was also pleased because I was supporting myself and even had a little extra money for some new clothes, a night out at the movies, and a cell phone (my big splurge over the weekend).

I was pleased that I had helped the accounting department get focused and energized through the power of a shared vision. I enjoyed the people I worked with and felt that the work we were doing was important. I also liked the company. And most important, my relationship with Jim had added dimension to my life. Jim brought out the best in me. And, he told me I brought out the best in him. I believed that as we figured out this 'vision thing,' the company would begin to sparkle and performance would skyrocket. Certainly, the sparkle was happening in the accounting department.

Early Monday, Jim and I were sitting quietly at the table, sipping coffee. I was sharing my reflections with Jim about how my life had changed for the positive since I had started working at the agency.

In the midst of our conversation, I was startled by the sound of a phone ringing. I looked at Jim, who looked back at me with a surprised expression. I realized there was no phone in the copy room. The sound was from my new cell phone at the bottom of my handbag. I rummaged through my bag, found the phone, and answered. It was my son Alex.

"Mom, don't be mad at me," he began. "I got in a fight with some boys on the way to school. I'm OK. I promise. I'm with a police officer right now. She wants to talk with you."

I caught my breath. *What was going on?*

"Your son seems OK," the officer said. "But he lost consciousness briefly, and he has a cut on his forehead. An ambulance is on the way. You can meet us at the hospital. I'd like to talk with you."

I felt a rising panic. I headed quickly out the door. Jim ran after me. "What's going on?" he asked.

"Alex is hurt. I'm going to the hospital."

"I'm coming along," Jim responded. "We'll take my car. You don't look like you should be driving."

He was right.

While Jim drove, I tried to calm down and told him the little I knew. He suggested that I call Doug, which I did. I couldn't reach him but left messages at home and at work. That was the best I could do.

When we arrived at the hospital, Alex and the police officer were already there. Alex was in a room waiting for a doctor. When he turned and looked at me, I gasped. He was holding a bloody rag over his eye.

"Mom," he said, starting to cry. I was so upset, I started to cry, too.

"What happened?" I asked.

Alex was too upset to talk. He wasn't making any sense. At that point the doctor came in and began to examine him. The cut was right above Alex's eye.

"It's not a bad cut, but it will require stitches," the doctor said calmly. "And because you lost consciousness, Alex, we'll need to observe you overnight."

Stay overnight in the hospital? What was going on?

The police officer asked me if I could step outside to speak with her a moment. Alex was being attended to by the nurse and seemed to have calmed down. I looked at Jim, who had been standing there the whole time, solid as a rock. He accompanied me out of the room.

The officer said, "Ma'am. From the report by the neighbor who called me—and as much as I can tell at this point—your son was involved in a fight with three boys. One of them hit him in the face with a rock. When he fell to the ground, the boys ran off. The neighbor found him dazed. Alex doesn't seem to remember much about the incident, but he told me that these boys have been harassing him for some time. I'd like to know what you've done about this situation so far."

I stood looking at her speechless. *What had I done about the situation? How could I have done anything about the situation when I didn't even know about the situation?* I told her that this was the first I was hearing about anything. She paused and looked me over. I figured she was appraising me as a mother, and I was coming up short. She said simply, "If you want to file a police report, you can call or come to the police station." She gave me her phone number and left.

I turned and looked at Jim, stunned. He put his arm around my shoulder and said, "One thing at a time, Ellie. Let's see how Alex is doing."

We went back in the room. The rest of the day was a whirlwind. A surgeon stitched and dressed the wound. Alex was moved to a different room. He was put in a hospital gown, and I was handed his bloody clothes. Jim headed back to work while I stayed at the hospital. Doug called. I explained what had happened. He said he'd stop by the hospital after work. Before I knew it, it was time to get Jen. All during this time, I had no time to talk with Alex about what had happened beyond the details of how his face was cut. I went to pick Jen up at school so she wouldn't come home to an empty house and wonder what was happening.

I told Jen what had happened to her brother. She was upset but, to my amazement, not surprised. Instead she said, "I figured something like this was going to happen sooner than later. Maybe now someone will do something." She sounded angry. I assumed she was angry with the boys who hurt Alex.

Doug said that Jen could sleep at his house so I could stay at the hospital that evening with Alex. I dropped Jen off at Doug's and went back to the hospital to stay with Alex. I tried to talk with him about what had happened, but he was uncommunicative. I thought he might be drowsy from medication or just exhausted by all the events, so I didn't press for information.

At bedtime, I headed home to an empty house feeling confused and overwhelmed. When I got home, there was a message on my answering machine, "Hi, Ellie, it's Jim. Call me at home when you get this message. It doesn't matter how late it is."

It felt so good to hear Jim's voice. All day I had focused on Alex and Jen. Doug had done his duty as a father, but he hadn't been there for me. And who would have expected him to be, anyway? He wasn't there when we were married. Why would he be there now? I didn't realize how lonely I was feeling until I heard Jim's kind voice on my machine.

I called the number, and a young woman answered. "I'm sorry, I think I may have dialed the wrong number.

"Are you Ellie?" she asked.

"Yes."

"I'm Kristen, Jim's daughter. Dad told me you'd probably call. I'm sorry to hear about your son."

She handed the phone to her father.

"How's Alex?"

The genuine concern in his voice allowed me to let down my guard. Through my tears I told him what I knew, which wasn't much.

"Ellie," Jim said. "I'm glad Alex is OK. I know this has been a really hard day for him and also for you. I'm also concerned about Jen."

"Jen?" I asked. "She's fine. She's at her father's place."

Then Jim said something that stopped me dead in my tracks.

"Ellie, you've got to take a look at what is going on at home. It's hard for me to say this, but I'm taking the risk because I care about you. I was watching you talk with Alex and later with the police officer. Clearly you love your children, but you seem out of touch with what they are experiencing. I think you need to have a serious talk with your children."

Hanging up the phone with Jim, I was struck by a blinding headache. I stumbled toward the medicine cabinet. As I glanced in the mirror, my vision blurred, and I could hardly see myself at all.

I spent much of the night awake, thinking about what was really going on at home and what I needed to do as a mother.

Sometimes, it's painful to look at the truth. It's easier to hold onto our illusions of what we want things to be or to hold onto our anger about changes that have been forced onto us. I realized that I had been doing both. I had been telling myself that the children were fine because they weren't complaining. And I realized that by holding onto my anger with

Doug, I could blame him for destroying our family
and absolve myself of the responsibility to rebuild
a new one. A good look in the mirror can be quite
a shock.

• • •

I picked up Alex at the hospital early the next morning. I had arranged to take the day off from work. Alex
was subdued as we drove home. I didn't say much on
the ride, either. Once home, I made him breakfast. As
we sat the table, I said, "Alex, I love you a lot. I'm not
sure how much I've been showing that to you lately. I
want to know what's going on because I care about
you and want to help you. Please tell me anything you
want to—about our family, about me as your mother,
about school, about the boys that you got in the fight
with. I want to listen and I'm here."

Suddenly a flood of words and thoughts and anger
filled the room. Alex opened up.

"You don't care about what happens to me anymore! All you care about is work! We're not a family
anymore. I'm really, really alone, and you just don't
care."

"I'm sorry, Alex. I'm sorry." I took his head in my
hands and drew him close. He began to sob.

When he was ready to talk, he said, "Some boys
started teasing me a couple of months ago. They
made fun of me because I was the only boy in my art
class. I stopped taking art lessons, but they didn't
stop teasing me. I tried to ignore them. But the
more I ignored them, the nastier they got.

Yesterday, I'd had enough. On my way to school, they followed me and called me names again. So instead of ignoring them, I called them names back. I used words you would never let me use, Mom. I thought that would stop them, but the next thing I knew, all three boys were on top of me beating me. I'm not even sure who hit me with the rock. I don't remember much after that. I think a woman ran out of a house, and the boys got scared and ran away. I think she called the police."

"Alex, why haven't you told me all of this was going on?"

He was silent for the longest moment, as if he were trying to avoid answering my question. I just waited, refusing to back down.

He finally said, "I've already told you, Mom. You're so busy with work all the time. Besides, I know you want me to handle my own problems. You have so many of your own problems that you just don't need any more."

I could have wept when I heard him say that. He was thinking it was his job to protect me. "Does anyone know that this has been going on?" I asked.

"Jen knows, but nobody else."

"That must be why she wasn't surprised when I told her what had happened," I suggested. "In fact, she seemed more angry than upset."

"I think she *is* angry, Mom."

It was starting to sink in just how badly I had been shirking my responsibilities as a mother.

"We have two problems to solve, Alex. One problem is with these bullies. No one expects you to solve this kind of problem alone. Your father and I need to help with the bullies. We'll file the police report and get the boys' parents involved. We'll also let the school know what happened. We're absolutely not going to allow any taunting or harassment to continue."

Alex looked relieved.

"The second problem is one that Jen, you, and I need to solve together. We need to talk about our family—about what has been happening to us and how we can make things better."

• • •

When Jen came home from school that afternoon, Alex and I were waiting for her with fresh-baked cookies and milk. I had had several hours to think about what was going on and decided that I needed to listen to the children. I announced that we needed to have a family meeting.

Jen really let me have it. She scorchingly, in no uncertain terms, told me what a rotten mother I had been. I could see that Alex was angry, too, although he hadn't expressed it as openly as Jen.

"Mom, it feels like you don't care about us anymore," Jen accused. "You don't cook meals anymore—you heat up macaroni and cheese from a box or order pizza. You're always gone in the morning before I wake up. You don't put me to bed anymore, tell me stories, or kiss me goodnight!"

I told Jen I hadn't realized how bad things had been for her and Alex and how really sorry I was. I hugged her, wiped her tears, and said, "Sweetheart, things are going to change now."

Jen sniffled, "I miss the stories you used to make up."

I had to acknowledge that Jen was right. I had really been blowing things. I had been feeling so much better at work but was ignoring the signals that things weren't better at home at all. My independent, self-reliant children really did need me, and I hadn't been there for them. I felt terrible.

The amazing thing about children is how resilient and forgiving they are. They're not nearly as hard on us as we are on ourselves. After a while, the accusations and tears began to diminish, and Jen let me take her in my arms.

• • •

After dinner, I broached the subject again with the children. "I've missed telling you stories. I'd like us to make up one together now—one about what kind of family we want to be. And then I'd like us to make it a true story."

We began to talk about our hopes and dreams for our family. We openly shared what we wanted from each other. We discussed why a family is important and what our purpose as a family is. We listed our most passionate values and explored how we hoped to act and how we wanted to be treated by each other. We talked about what really pushes our buttons or violates our core values.

Then we each answered the question "What do I care deeply about?" We created a picture of what it would look like if we were really being the kind of family we wanted to be. We talked about what our relationships would look like, how we would feel about each other, how we would feel about ourselves, what we would be doing, what we would be saying, what our home would look like, what kinds of activities we would do together, and what things we would prefer to do alone. We shared many pictures of what an ideal future would look like.

The more we talked, the more I realized that it was all possible. We didn't need a father in our home to be a family. But we did need to be clear about our vision.

After the children went to bed, I wrote up a statement that summarized what we had discussed. Later, as I prepared for bed, I realized the headache that had plagued me for most of the day was gone. I glanced in the mirror and saw a clear reflection smiling back at me.

At breakfast, I showed the statement to the children. They really liked it. They made a few changes, but the essence remained the same.

Our purpose as a family is to support each others' growth and to contribute to our community. Our values are love, respect, open communication, learning, and fun. We know we are acting on our values when we honor the right of each of us to be who we are, when we speak the truth in a way that others can hear, when we encourage each other to look at things in a new way, and when we play together and laugh. Our mom is a constant force in our lives.

We can depend on her. She is aware of how we are doing in school and expects the best of us. She is a role model for us as a loving mother, a working parent, and someone we can confide in. Jen and Alex contribute to the welfare of our family. We do our chores without being reminded because we depend on each other. We support each other's growth by encouraging each other to be the best we can be. We contribute to worthy causes with donations and volunteer our time. We dance, tell stories, and play cards together. We're not perfect, and we don't want to be. But we learn from our mistakes. Sometimes we argue, but we always make up, because our love is stronger than anything. As we grow older and our lives change, our love will always unite us and our dreams will always guide us.

I put it on our refrigerator to keep it as visible as possible.

• • •

We had done it! We had created a family vision— significant purpose, clear values, and pictures of what we wanted to become, what it looks like when our purpose and values are being fulfilled. And because it was a shared vision, I knew we were all on the same boat together, able to move full steam ahead. What a relief!

I was so proud of us. There was just one problem. One of the key points in the vision was that I was a constant force in their lives. At this still-young age, it meant they needed to see me in the morning before they left for school. And that meant I wouldn't be able to continue meeting Jim in the morning. I really didn't want to give up that special time with him. So that piece wasn't feeling too good.

But I was absolutely certain: My family is—and has to be—the most important thing in my life. Period.

You Can't Get to the Future without Being Present

I didn't go in early to work that day. Later in the morning, I sent Jim an e-mail thanking him for his help and telling him briefly about my conversation with my children. I also said that I'd like to talk with him, couldn't come in early, and asked him to call me at home after work.

That evening, Jim and I had a long talk on the phone. I told him in detail about my conversations with my children, how I had taken a hard look in the mirror at myself as a mother, and about our new family vision. He was supportive and impressed. We agreed that an important part of having a vision was to be honest about the current realities. In fact, an honest and accurate assessment of the present is as important as a vision of the future. They go together. Jim made me laugh when he said, "You can't get to the future without being present."

How true! I thought of Marsha, who was incredibly excited about the accounting department since we had identified a shared vision. She saw good things beginning to happen. But there were also some problems cropping up that she was ignoring. One of the people in our department was dropping the ball, and no one was confronting him. Everyone just worked around him, but it made things harder for the rest of us—and didn't seem right. It occurred to me that unless our department did an honest and accurate assessment of our current situation, we would never be able to fully achieve our vision. That's what happens when you focus on the future without also looking at the present.

And then I thought about the opposite kind of situation—where people focus on the present without a vision for the future. Immediately, my ex-husband Doug came to mind. His focus was on the things that were wrong in the present. Because of that, all he did was complain or react. He was totally stuck in the present. In addition, he couldn't even honestly look at his role in our problems. Because of this viewpoint, he was unable to be proactive and create his desired future. Instead, he just gave up.

I decided that both of these views are important: a clear vision for the future and an honest view of the present. Vision without being present is like having your head in the clouds. Holding the present without vision is like being stuck in the mud.

I had reflected for such a long time that Jim finally asked, "Are you there?"

"Yes, I am." I replied. "More here than I've ever been. It just hit me like a ton of bricks.

"As your vision becomes clear, you have to look at your current reality and take stock. You have to be honest with yourself—which is hard to do if you're blaming yourself or someone else. You have to put the blame away. It's not helpful because it keeps you from seeing the truth.

"But you have to do both—you have to maintain your focus on your vision, and you have to be honest about the truth of your present."

"You're right!" Jim responded. "I'm reminded of the *Titanic*. Now that was a powerful steamship! It was designed, developed, and launched with a clear vision of being the largest, most luxurious, strongest steamship ever. They were totally focused on their vision. But they were unprepared for the possibility of unforeseen forces. They didn't hold an honest account of their present realities. Aware of the icebergs, they made a terrible decision to hold to a time line while denying the danger of their current situation. The disastrous result is an example of focusing on the vision without looking at the present at the same time.

"Doing both—focusing on your vision and being honest about the truth of your present situation is what allows you to move full steam ahead. That means that the moment your vision becomes conscious, you have to start living it. Even as your vision is forming, you need to act on what you know. You have to bring your vision into your present."

"So, vision isn't just about the future, is it? It's about the present," I said.

"Absolutely," my good friend replied. And then he said something that struck me:

> *Learn from the past,*
> *plan for the future, and*
> *live in the present.*
> *In other words: Live your vision now.*

"If I live my family's vision now," I said, "it means no more early-morning talks for us. I'm just worried about how this change in my routine will affect our relationship. Our morning conversations have meant so much to me. It's such a special time, and it really helps me start my day on a good note. I hate to give that time up. Realistically, though, I know that I need to be there for my children. That morning time is important to them, too."

I was hoping that Jim would come up with an alternative.

As usual, he answered me directly.

"Ellie, our conversations have added a lot to both our lives and are important to both of us. I don't like the idea of giving up our morning time together, either, because it's such a perfect time for me, too. I do agree that your children come first. What if you had a family meeting with them and told them about our conversations and how important they have been to you? Would they be willing to let you come in early one morning a week? That might be a possible solution."

I agreed to talk with them. I knew that I would need to make sure they would be honest with me. Since honesty was part of our family vision, I could begin the conversation by reviewing the vision—that would set the stage for an open, honest problem-solving discussion. I could see that the family vision was going to be important for helping our family go forward.

Then Jim had an interesting thought. "I've been thinking about Alex. You mentioned that he likes to draw but doesn't want to take art class right now because no other boys are in the class."

"That's right," I replied. "I really see him struggling with how much of his gentler side he wants to show. I think this thing with the bullies has made him feel he needs to show a tougher side."

"It would be a shame for him not to develop his talent," Jim continued. "My daughter, Kristen, will be home for the summer. She'll be working part-time at the agency in marketing. I think you know she's an art major. She might enjoy giving Alex some private art lessons. She's been a camp counselor in the past and has always enjoyed being with younger children, maybe because she doesn't have any siblings of her own. Do you think that might be a good idea?"

"It's a wonderful idea! Our family's vision says that we support each others' growth. This is a creative alternative that allows Alex to continue developing his

art abilities and takes the pressure off while he's working out his issues with his image. Let's talk with Alex
and Kristen and see what they think of the idea."

What an amazing thing about having a vision, I
thought. *If you are clear about your vision, and if you are
honest about your present realities, you don't have to figure
everything out. Things start happening of their own accord.
What a gift!* I felt so grateful.

The children agreed that I could go into work
early one morning a week as long as it wasn't Monday.
They wanted me home for the beginning of the week.
Jim and I chose Tuesday as "our morning" and thus
began a routine of weekly conversations.

Kristen did give art lessons to Alex that summer
and their relationship bloomed. She was an amazing
young woman and a wonderful "big sister" to Alex,
who really needed and benefited from her guidance
and friendship.

20/20 Vision

Our Tuesday morning discussions became more focused. Jim was considering his vision for the agency. At the same time, I was working on my vision for my life.

I had gotten to know Jim and his family much better. Alex was at Jim's house frequently visiting Kristen. During the transitions of dropping Alex off and picking him up, I often chatted with Jim's wife Carolyn. One afternoon, as I waited for Alex, Carolyn confided in me, "I know you and Jim are talking about vision. This is so important for him. Until he creates his own vision for the agency, he'll always be living in his father's shadow."

One Tuesday morning, shortly after my conversation with Carolyn, Jim and I were chatting about vision. Reflecting on my marriage, I remarked, "I think it was easy to have a vision when the sun was shining and everything was going right. I thought I knew where I was going and was on the right path.

We married, had children, and lived our lives. I didn't even consider what my vision was. Everything was going according to plan."

Jim watched in respectful silence as I struggled to put my thoughts into words. After a moment, I continued, "I'm not the kind of person who reflects a lot on life. I just live it. That worked fine until I hit a brick wall. When Doug walked out, I was hurt and confused. I blamed him and I blamed myself. But the truth is I hadn't been happy, either; I just hadn't admitted it to myself.

"If I had been clear about my vision or if Doug and I had shared a vision, we could have talked about what we were doing that was consistent with our vision and where we were off track. Maybe we could have fixed things early on before they became irreparable."

We sat quietly, each lost in our own thoughts. After a moment, Jim broke the silence saying, "The same is true for me. I always knew that someday I would take over the business from my father. Everyone in my family wanted it, and I think I wanted it, too. Or at least I never considered anything else. So, maybe that was a vision. But it wasn't a clear vision—because here I am now, president of the company, and I can't seem to make it shine the way my father did. A vision should guide you. I feel like I'm going one step at a time, but I'm not sure where it's leading."

I smiled at Jim. I was touched by his frankness and honesty, and I remembered what Carolyn had said. *Maybe Carolyn is right*, I thought. I decided to push him gently.

"I've been thinking about what we've discovered about vision. We've identified three elements to a compelling vision: Significant Purpose, Clear Values, and a Picture of the Future. We know these elements need to be clearly understood in order for the vision to provide clarity and inspire commitment. Jim, I think you *do* know what your vision is. You've already told me what you believe these three elements are for the agency. I think you just haven't put them all to-gether yet. Here's what I mean.

"The first week I met you, you told me the pur-pose of your agency. Remember? You said you were in the 'peace of mind' business—that the agency pro-vided customers with financial security for possible worst-case scenarios and security in knowing they will be supported if they need to place a claim. Right?"

"That's right," Jim replied evenly. "It's something I learned from my father."

"Do you believe it, yourself?" I asked.

"Absolutely. Knowing we have a worthwhile pur-pose motivates me to work in the family business."

"OK. And during our time together, you've al-ready identified the values you believe are needed to guide people as they pursue that purpose, right?"

"Right, again," Jim replied, looking at me curi-ously. "The values are *ethics, relationships,* and *success.*"

I took a breath and pushed on, "So just tell me right now—what would it look like, what would you see if we, if everyone in the agency, were living this purpose and values consistently? I'm listening."

I paused and waited, hoping that Jim would take this as a challenge and not be offended.

Jim chuckled and said, "OK, Ellie. I'll tell you."

I sat there and listened while Jim shared the pictures of a possible future for his agency with me.

"My vision is that we really deliver on peace of mind—every single time for every single customer. It means we develop trust-based relationships with our customers. We help them choose the best products for their specific situation; and when they need to make a claim, they only need to make one call—to us. We make it happen. It also means that we create that same atmosphere within our agency—peace of mind. It means that every department and every individual is clear about how they contribute to our vision. It means that we can trust each other to follow through on commitments, that we will treat each other with mutual respect—which means being clear about our roles and holding ourselves and each other accountable. It means that we are committed to working through disagreements with our customer in mind, and not our egos. It means that we are knowledgeable and competent in negotiating the most benefits for the lowest price for our customers and that we provide unparalleled service for our customers as their advocates in settling claims.

"If we do this, our customers will be our number one marketers; 100 percent will recommend us to their friends and relatives. Our agency will be recognized by the city as an important contributor to our community. Every single person who works here will come to work each day, enthusiastic about being here."

Jim waited for my reaction. I was absolutely blown away.

"Jim," I said excitedly. "You included everything—purpose, values, and a picture of the future. And it works! How do you feel?"

"Amazed. No, energized! It really *is* what I want for the agency. You were right. I knew it all along," Jim declared. "I feel like I'm moving full steam ahead!"

"Well, that's what we said a vision would do!" I laughed. "And guess what, I feel energized, too! I want to be in the same boat. There's a lot of steam power in your vision!"

We sat quietly, basking in the joy of discovery.

As we headed off to work that morning, Jim said thoughtfully, "I think I'll just sit with this a while before I do anything."

Jim didn't bring up the subject of his vision again for several weeks. I suspected that he was spending time considering it, testing his commitment or possibly just imagining it more deeply.

• • •

Over the next few weeks, we focused on my personal vision. Now that I had seen the power of a shared vision for my family, I was more motivated than ever to create a vision for myself. By creating a family vision, I found a tremendous amount of energy was suddenly freed up—no more sluggish weekends.

However, I didn't have much of a social life outside home and work; and although I loved working at the agency, I had to admit that my job in the accounting department was not satisfying.

I had figured out this much: My vision needed to be about the *quality* of the life I wanted to live, and not about the specifics. I had a friend who was sure she would never be fulfilled unless she could find the right husband. Another friend was certain she would never be fulfilled unless she had children. Another friend believed that he would never be fulfilled unless he got a Ph.D. I noticed that people got attached to specific goals as though they not only *represented* the vision but *were* the vision. And this confused them.

Of course, this was easier to see in others than in myself.

• • •

One Tuesday morning, I opened our conversation on the subject of values.

"I know that if I want to create a vision, I need to be clear about my values. The values of the agency make sense to me and guide me at work, but are these the same as my personal values?"

"No," Jim replied. "The values of the agency work for you because they are aligned with your personal values. That's why you fit in here so well. But your personal values reflect what *you* care most deeply about."

"I remember how impressed I was when you shared your values during a voicemail message. How did you identify them?" I asked.

"That's not difficult. We all know what our values are, whether we've spent the time to put them into words or not. You might ask yourself questions such as, 'What do I care deeply about?' or 'What do I stand for?' See what comes up. The more deeply you care, the closer you are to your core values."

"I don't think it's as easy as you make it sound, Jim" I replied.

"OK, here are three questions. Pick one and answer it. *One.* Think of an important decision you had to make, and then identify the things you considered as you made it. *Two.* Think of something you're proud of, at work or in your personal relationships. *Three.* Imagine a risky situation. What would make you move forward rather than avoid it?"

"OK," I said, taking the challenge. "I pick number 3. A risky situation would be telling a co-worker that she had hurt my feelings."

"What's risky about that?" Jim queried.

"I'd be concerned that we might not be able to resolve the conflict and she'd avoid me in the future."

"What would make you take the risk? What would make you tell her she had hurt your feelings?" Jim asked.

I thought for a moment and then replied, "If I was fairly certain that she cared about me and would want to resolve it."

"Sounds like you value relationships," Jim remarked.

That didn't fit exactly for me. I really didn't value all relationships. I didn't have lots of friends. I had a few close friends, and I loved my family dearly. These were the relationships that mattered to me. Then I got it.

"I value *loving* relationships, not just relationships in general," I responded, realizing that I had tapped into one of my core values.

I spent the rest of the week asking myself, *What do I really value? When I get down to the core, what really matters most to me? What is absolutely essential to who I am? What do I stand for?* I thought of a friend who seemed to value money. He might even say that money was a value for him. I wondered whether that was really a value or whether the accumulation of wealth represented a deeper value. Power, perhaps? Status? Achievement? Control over his destiny? I guessed that only he could answer that for himself.

Through my continued discussions with Jim, I became aware of three values that I held most dearly—*loving relationships, truth,* and *creative expression.*

I also identified my purpose: *to listen to the world around me, including the ideas, hopes, and dreams of myself and others, in order to create understanding and clarity in expression.*

One morning, I sat with Jim and read to him the last piece—my picture of the future:

In loving myself, I open myself to loving relationships. My true power and sense of self-worth comes from within me. Although it is a joy when I can share my deepest experiences with another, I am not dependent on others to help me fulfill my purpose. I keep healthy mentally, emotionally, and physically.

I move toward the truth to listen and witness. The world reveals itself. I hear hopes and dreams, ideas and beliefs—my own and others'. Through listening, I help myself and others bring their dreams to a conscious level in order to creatively express them. I am not the center of the universe but an instrument of life creatively expressing itself.

Jim looked at me dumbfounded.

"This is your vision statement?" he asked.

"Yes," I replied, proudly.

"It's beautiful. But I don't get it. I thought a vision should create a picture of what it looks like in the future when your purpose and values are being fulfilled."

"It doesn't matter whether *you* can see the picture. It's *my* vision. It's a picture that I can see," I countered.

I then went on to explain some of the thinking that went into my vision. "One of the lessons I learned when my marriage ended was how much of my identity was caught up in being a wife and mother. When Doug left, I felt like I was nobody, almost like I really didn't exist. I've grown a lot since I met you and we started working on vision. This vision statement doesn't describe exactly where I am now, but it does describe how I want to be and what I believe I am moving toward—someone whose sense of self-worth is not dependent on others. And at the same time, someone who is not so totally self-sufficient that there's no room for others.

"I wrote this in present tense, instead of future tense," I continued, "so I could see it happening now. It energizes me and provides me focus. Maybe that's the difference between a personal vision and a vision that involves others, such as a family vision or an organizational vision. It doesn't need to provide focus or direction for anyone other than yourself."

"Ellie, you always like to do things you own way," Jim laughed. "And when I think of it, your vision is aligned with your values: loving relationships, truth, and creative expression. In fact, your entire vision statement *is* a creative expression. And if it works for you, I respect it. I also suspect that as the years pass, the more you will refine it."

"Maybe," I answered. "And I imagine that there are probably a lot of ways to express a personal vision."

"You remind me of a story I read about Alfred Nobel, father of the Nobel Peace Prize," Jim commented. "When his brother died, Nobel picked up a Swedish newspaper to see what they had written about him. The paper had gotten the two brothers confused, so Alfred Nobel read his own obituary instead. Alfred Nobel was one of the inventors of dynamite, so his obituary was all about dynamite and destruction.

He was just devastated. Later, when his friends and loved ones gathered, Alfred asked them, 'What do you think is the opposite of destruction?' They all agreed it was peace. Right then he decided to chart a new course for his life so he would be remembered for peace."

"So an obituary could be an expression of a vision," I remarked.

"It could," Jim replied thoughtfully.

• • •

The next morning, Jim handed me a typed page.

"Read this," he said with a smile.

He had written his own obituary! I read it with interest.

Jim Carpenter was a loving teacher and example of simple truths, whose leadership helped himself and others awaken the presence of God in their lives. He was a caring child of God, a son, brother, spouse, father, grandfather, father-in-law, brother-in-law, godfather, uncle, cousin, friend, and business colleague, who strove to find a balance between success and significance. He had a spiritual peace about him that permitted him to say no in a loving manner to people and projects that got him off purpose. He was a person of high energy who was able to see the positive in any event or situation. No matter what happened, he could find a "learning" or a message in it. Jim Carpenter was someone who trusted God's unconditional love and believed he was truly the beloved.

He valued integrity, his actions were consistent with his words, and he was a mean, lean, 185-pound, flexible golfing machine. He will be missed because wherever he went, he made the world a better place by his having been there.

"Guess you're going to have to start working on your golf game," I teased. "Sounds like you're doing pretty well with the rest."

"I put the golf game in because it symbolizes that I maintain my health and my physical abilities and that I enjoy sports."

"Your pictures created meaning for you—just like mine did for me," I concluded.

"You're right," Jim responded. "My personal vision might not inspire or have meaning for anyone else, but it does for me.

"I've been thinking about your personal vision some more," he continued. "It's clear that your talents and interest lie more in creative expression than in the world of numbers. Why do you work in the accounting department?"

I explained to Jim that I actually didn't like working with numbers, even though I was good with them. I had gotten a college degree in business because I thought it would give me security. I had gotten the job in the accounting department for the same reason. It was something I knew how to do, and I was desperate for financial security immediately after my divorce. I told Jim that I didn't look for a different job because I loved working for the agency.

"The bottom line is, I don't want to leave the agency," I concluded glumly.

"I think you should talk with Marsha about your concerns. I hear there's an opening in the marketing department. It would be a good fit with your talents, especially since you understand the purpose of our business so well."

Within a few weeks, I was working in the marketing department. It meant starting at the bottom doing mostly copyediting and formatting, but I was learning things that would help me further develop my real talents and passion. I was thrilled!

• • •

I was discovering the power of being clear about my vision and honest about the present. When I was able to do both these things, opportunities seemed to appear almost as if by magic. Of course, admitting the truth about the present made me uncomfortable. It had been painful to acknowledge that I had fallen short in my role as a mother; it was easier to deny that it was happening or to blame Doug.

By being clear about what was important and being honest about the present, I was able to make a shift. My family was better off now than ever.

The same had been true for my work. I had not wanted to be honest with myself that I wasn't happy in the accounting department because I was afraid it would mean I'd have to look for another employer and I'd lose my relationship with Jim.

But, as I maintained my focus on what was important and also what was real, an unexpected opportunity in the marketing department had surfaced. These shifts came about because of my willingness to experience and live with the tension generated from focusing on both my vision and the truth about the present.

At times the tension of holding both an honest view of the present and my vision was painful. It felt like jumping off a cliff, with no assurance of any landing, let alone a safe landing.

One of the lessons I had learned from Doug helped me remember the importance of not resisting the tension or fear. Early in our marriage, I had joined Doug on his fishing expeditions. I had noticed that when hooked on a line, the fish usually pulls against the tension of the line. The fisherman plays this game with the fish, letting the line out and pulling it in until the fish is worn out and then easily reeled in. But sometimes a smart fish doesn't play this game. The smart fish swims toward the pole keeping the tension loose until it finds a way to get off the hook. I was learning to be like the smart fish—to swim toward the hook instead of away from it. By resisting the truth about my current reality, I had been getting worn out and was losing the opportunity to create my desired future. I discovered that by being honest about my present, accepting the tension or uncomfortable feelings, and also focusing on my vision at the same time, ultimately a shift occurs.

My present reality slowly began to move toward my vision.

A New Contract:
From Vision to Reality

W̲e had achieved what we had initially agreed to do.
We had figured out the "vision thing." We were both
pleased with what we had accomplished.

One Tuesday morning, we sat quietly looking at
each over our cups of coffee.

"Are we finished?" I asked. "We've identified the
three elements of a compelling vision. You've figured
out your vision for the agency. And we've both gotten
clear on our vision for our personal lives."

"It's one thing to identify the vision. It's another to
make it happen," Jim remarked thoughtfully. "I don't
feel like the agency is ready to move full steam ahead.
No one is on the boat with me yet. Now I have to
figure out how to get others to see it, want to join, and
figure out how to make the vision come alive. Seems
like we have more work to do, Ellie. Are you up for it?"

I smiled. "I can't think of another way I'd rather
spend my Tuesday mornings."

And so we began a new contract for another
piece of work—moving from vision to reality.

We knew that creating an appealing vision was not enough. Our motto was:

*Vision is a lot more than putting a plaque on the wall.
A real vision is lived, not framed.*

We decided to identify the things that were important to consider in creating a shared vision.

As we reflected further, I thought about the vision I had created with my children for our family. It struck me that the discussions we had in shaping the vision were as powerful as the vision itself. If I had presented to my children the exact same vision without involving them in creating it, I doubted that it would have meant as much to them. It occurred to me that Jim needed to involve others as he shaped his vision for his agency.

"I don't think you can just go out and announce your new vision and expect everyone to immediately understand it or agree," I commented. "You need to look at who should be involved in shaping the vision, and you have to be open to their thoughts, dreams, hopes and needs. You have to be willing to allow them to help shape it."

"You're right," Jim agreed. "So 'how it's created' is important."

Jim continued, "I also think how it's communicated is important. Even if people aren't involved in shaping it, they need to understand it so they can act in support of it."

He then took out an piece of notepaper and wrote the following:

FOR VISION TO BECOME A REALITY, WHAT'S IMPORTANT IS

- How it's created

- How it's communicated

- How it's lived

He placed this piece of notepaper on the wall above the other three notepapers describing each of the elements of a compelling vision and the rest of the cards in our "road map."

Jim smiled and said, "For the past six months, since we've begun our conversations, we've worked on identifying the elements of a compelling vision. We've done a great job. But it's not enough. For our visions to become a reality, we need to figure out the 'Three Hows.'"

"So we can move full steam ahead, all on the same boat," I smiled back.

How It's Created

It was Tuesday morning, and we sat comfortably drinking coffee. Jim announced, "I'm ready to share my vision with others in the agency. Here's my question. How much do I allow them to have input? I'm pretty passionate about it. I'm not thrilled about the idea that they might change it substantially."

I thought about the vision of Martin Luther King Jr. It really wasn't just his vision alone. By the time he expressed it, he had talked with and heard from thousands. His vision expressed the hopes and dreams of millions of people.

"I think your job as the leader of this company is to help articulate the vision, to champion the vision, but not to 'own' the vision," I offered. "Everyone in the company must own the vision. Otherwise, it's just *your* vision and not a *shared* vision."

"I need to share my vision with others and then be open to hearing their thoughts and reactions. What you're saying is I also need to be open to including their hopes and dreams in shaping it," Jim replied as he considered what I had said.

"Exactly," I agreed.

Jim shrugged, "I guess you're right. The reality is that if there's something in my vision that they don't agree with, it doesn't matter how passionate I am—it won't happen anyway."

"You still sound reluctant. Here's what I think. You're impressed by what Marsha did with the accounting department. Why don't you talk more with her about how she accomplished it?" I suggested.

Marsha told Jim her department's vision was compelling, even though the agency itself did not have a clear vision. It was obvious to everyone that the people in her department were energized and enthusiastic about what they wanted to accomplish. Marsha said that vision was a unifying force for her department and also helped them focus on what was important. Marsha told Jim that they had created the vision together—that she didn't create the vision alone. She said she had created an opportunity and environment where people were able to honestly share their hopes and dreams for the future. Through that discussion, they discovered the common threads and developed the shared vision together.

Through his discussions with Marsha, Jim discovered the principle of *How It's Created:*

➡ **The process of creating the vision is as important as what the vision says.**

Jim knew that he could not be the "glue" for the company the way his father had been. He wanted the vision to be the glue.

So this is what he did. Instead of simply taking the top management off on a retreat to put the vision together and then announcing the vision, he encouraged dialogue about the vision. Everyone in the agency engaged in some type of dialogue and gave feedback on the vision.

In the beginning, some people were skeptical. Some said, "We've already done this stuff, and it's a waste of time." Others said, "Wait him out, and then things will get back to normal." Maybe they were concerned that they might have to change or lose something. What they didn't realize was how absolutely and totally committed Jim was to this process. Eventually they got the message.

Jim encouraged everyone to voice their concerns. He wanted all voices to be heard. He also had patience. He also knew that some people were holding back because they were uncomfortable. They weren't sure what to expect and had never had discussions like this before. He let them find their own way to join in.

The majority of us sincerely engaged in the dialogues right from the start. Those in Marsha's department were especially enthusiastic, as they saw this as a way to connect their vision for their department to the agency's vision. And as people got the message that Jim and the senior leaders were open to these discussions, more and more people became honestly engaged.

A momentum built. The more we shared our hopes and dreams, the more excited we became.

Seeing the difference between what we wanted and where we currently were, some people wanted to start making changes right away in order to fix the problems.

In our Tuesday conversations, Jim told me he had decided not to act quickly. In his opinion, most of the suggestions for changes, such as reorganization, were not well thought out and were simply an attempt to alleviate the tension that was building. Jim decided to encourage people to live with the tension, as they continued to take an honest look at their present realities and discuss their hopes and dreams for the future.

During those months, it was hard for Jim and many others to not take quick action. However, they did take action on "low-hanging fruit" —obvious things that could easily and quickly be changed. But the more serious issues with larger implications were studied during that period, so that they were more fully understood.

Some changes happened naturally. A few people decided that the vision didn't fit with their personal goals or with their beliefs of where the agency should be going. They left the agency. Others who had been resistant at first became enthusiastic leaders once they realized that the ship was really moving full steam ahead.

Through our sincere conversations about the future of the agency, we were creating a shared view of our desired future. Jim joined the conversations and shared his views actively, in person and through his voicemail messages. The voicemail system was very active during this period. Most of Jim's morning messages those months were dedicated to the vision—sharing both his views and the views of others. Because everyone was involved in some way in the discussions shaping the vision, once it was finalized, it was easy to communicate it. Everyone already understood it and had a deep sense of ownership for it.

By then, every department in the agency had started working on their own vision. They were able to create visions that were aligned with the vision for the agency. Things were really starting to shift, and Jim had begun to see the energy and sparkle he had been looking for!

How It's Communicated

One morning Jim and I were chatting about the value of condensing the huge amount of information in a vision statement into a rallying call.

"How can anyone ever remember everything that's in the vision statement unless they carry it with them everywhere?" Jim wondered.

"I think some people in Marsha's department do," I replied. "I remember a couple of times when we had to make tough decisions and they pulled it out to see where it could give them some guidance."

"I can see the value of creating a one-line rallying call that creates a short cut and helps the people in the organization remember what the vision is about. Like with Martin Luther King Jr.'s speech. All you have to say is 'I have a dream,' and it evokes images of the entire vision."

"I know what you mean," I replied.

"Do you recall the old commercials for Ford Motor Company when they were beginning to seriously compete with Japan?" I asked.

"I sure do," he responded. "'Quality is job one.'"

I continued. "I grew up in Michigan, so I'm very aware of the automotive industry. I was impressed with their rallying call 'Quality is job one.' To most people this sounds like they're saying, 'Quality is the most important job.' And they are. But it's also a message that conveys deeper meaning. Most people don't know this, but *job one* is the term for the prototype of each model—the first car off the assembly line. This car has to be perfect because it is the standard against which all of the other cars are built. When workers at Ford Motor first heard 'Quality is job one,' what they really heard was that every car they produced had to be perfect, held to the standard of the first job—the first car off the assembly line. They had a clear picture of what quality looks like. The rallying call also told them that they are going to seriously compete with the Japanese market in the area of quality. There was a lot of meaning attached to their rallying call, and it connected them to a shared vision. That was the year that the Ford Taurus overtook the Honda Accord as the best-selling car in that class."

"I remember when that happened," Jim responded. "The Japanese cars had dominated the market until that time. It was a huge turning point. Ford's vision allowed them to go full steam ahead!"

"But what happened?" I wondered. "It lasted for a while, but it doesn't seem to fit anymore."

"I'm not sure that vision guides them anymore," Jim replied. "And that can be a problem. If you lose sight of the vision or stop acting in concert with it, the rallying call becomes meaningless and actually turns people off."

"So you need to be sure that the rallying call really describes the shared vision. It needs to speak to the people in the organization to help them remember the vision—not just be a marketing message."

"Right," Jim continued. "I think a company could get into trouble if a leadership team was excited about a vision that wasn't shared throughout the company— yet they created a rallying call. Instead of exciting people, the rallying call might have the opposite effect of reminding people that the leadership is discon- nected from the rest of the organization, and it might actually demotivate them."

We agreed that a rallying call is a great way to encapsulate the messages of a shared vision. We thought of examples where the rallying call of a com- pany was a true expression of their vision, such as Ritz-Carlton's "We are ladies and gentlemen serving ladies and gentlemen" and Disney's "to keep the same smiles on people's faces when they leave the park that they had when they entered six, eight, or twelve hours earlier," and Steve Jobs's vision to make computers accessible and affordable for everyone by creating a world with "a computer on every desk."

• • •

The next Tuesday morning, Jim came in all excited. He announced with a broad smile, "I've been thinking more about the problem with Ford's 'Quality is job one.' Visioning is not a static process. You do not create a vision once and then stop. Visions are ongoing and continue to evolve. As you listen to others, your own vision will crystallize even further. This is why the ongoing communication is so important."

I reflected on what he was saying. It resonated as absolutely true. I thought about how our vision for our family was continuing to evolve as the children grew older.

We had uncovered the principle of *How It's Communicated:*

➤ **Visioning is an ongoing process; you need to keep talking about it.**

It's important to keep talking about the vision and refer to it as much as possible, because as you focus on the vision, the clearer it becomes and the more deeply you understand it. In fact, an aspect of what you thought was the vision may change over time, but the essence of it will remain.

Jim realized that communication of the vision was one of his most important jobs as a leader. He not only used the voicemail system but encouraged other leaders to do the same with their departments. We noticed that leaders were around a lot, talking informally about the vision and the strategies.

And written information was published in weekly communications.

. . .

We realized that one of the most important aspects of communication was to help people interpret events in light of the vision. At one point there was a downturn in the economy. Business was down. People were worried. Did this mean we were going under? During this period, Jim shared information with us on a regular basis that demonstrated that although we were cutting back in some areas, our vision was still the driving force for our agency. Leaders decided to focus on building stronger relationships with commercial customers, while maintaining the personal relationships with individual customers. He explained how this strategy was positioning us to move full steam ahead. It made sense. Communication around current events in relation to our vision allowed us to understand how we were continuing to move forward during adverse times and helped us stay committed.

How It's Lived

Jim and I discovered that "How It's Lived" is both the simplest and the hardest part of transforming a vision into reality. Once we identified our vision, we had to start living it immediately. We had to begin behaving consistently with the intention of our vision. Once we knew the right thing to do, we couldn't wait to start—we had to do the best we could with what we knew, using the abilities we had at that moment.

As soon as I realized I had been ignoring my children's needs, I had to stop. As soon as I agreed to be home with my children in the mornings, I had to begin. I couldn't say, "I'll start being a better mother next week."

That wasn't easy, because sometimes it meant making tough decisions. But I learned that the best thing for myself, my children, my friends, and my co-workers was to live my values and to make choices based on them.

In the agency, as we were still in the midst of dialogue about our vision, each of us had to start acting on our vision as it became clear. We needed to treat each other with respect and hold ourselves and each other accountable. Marsha realized she hadn't confronted the person in our department who had been dropping the ball. When she realized this, she had to act. She had to provide the leadership needed to help him focus on the priorities. She couldn't continue to ignore the problem. That was hard for her because it wasn't her style. But she set out clear expectations and consequences and worked with him to ensure that he met his responsibilities.

When a vision is shared, it is important to hold each other accountable for behaving consistently with it. If you ignore the behavior of others who act inconsistently with the vision, you threaten the trust and commitment of the people who are.

We discovered the importance of *supporting structures*: the habits, practices, and processes that support your vision. We need to establish structures that support the consistent practice of our values as we pursue our vision. Otherwise, our commitments fade into simply good intentions.

Once the accounting department was energized around a shared vision, Marsha had begun to put structures in place. The structures included goals, accountability, and team meetings. We had each written clear goals that we had shared with one another. We each knew the others' responsibilities and understood how we needed to work together to support each other and coordinate our work. Marsha met regularly with each of us to review our goals and discuss how things were going. If we were having trouble, she would meet more often with us and provide the direction and support we needed. If we didn't follow through on commitments, we were held accountable. Marsha set up regular team meetings to review our progress on shared goals, look at upcoming projects and decide how to coordinate our efforts, to solve problems, and to hold each other mutually accountable.

As these structures were put into place, I assumed that the person in our department who had been slacking off would either quit or be fired. I was surprised to see him get refocused and become a productive member of the team.

One Tuesday morning, about nine months after I had joined the agency, Jim was complaining about his increasing lack of stamina and recent weight gain. He attributed it to the effects of aging. I listened sympathetically for a while and then said, "Jim, I know that one of your values is health. You've talked about it several times in your morning messages. What is your exercise program?"

"Exercise program?" he asked.

"Yes," I chided. "What structure do you have in place that supports your value of health? I know you eat healthy food, so that structure is in place. And I know you play golf any chance you can get. But I'm not sure what you do regularly for exercise."

He sheepishly admitted that he had tried several different approaches to exercise but lost interest in them because they weren't fun, or he was too busy, or it wasn't convenient. I pointed out that these all sounded like excuses. He admitted that they were.

"Is health really a value?" I asked. "Or is it just an interest?"

He replied, "Yes, it's a value, and I'm feeling bad that I'm not acting consistently with it."

Then I had a great idea. "I'm not doing well in the exercise department, either. Maybe we could set up a structure that would help both of us. Instead of talking over coffee on Tuesday mornings, how about if we walked together?"

As a result, we set up a structure that supported our value of health, and we held each other accountable. Our Tuesday morning routine shifted once again as we continued our conversations during a brisk forty-five-minute walk.

I liked these walks so much that I started walking with Marsha a couple of days a week during our lunch break. Marsha and I had become good friends, especially now that she wasn't my boss anymore. This structure of walking together allowed us not only to get exercise but also to maintain and build on our friendship.

I enrolled in a writing course at our community college so that I could improve my skills. Jim encouraged me to set up a structure to support my writing, so I bought a journal and wrote for twenty minutes each night before going to bed.

Setting up structures that supported our vision was also important in the agency. Some of the policies and procedures were antiquated and made getting the job done harder instead of easier. We reexamined almost all of the agency's policies and procedures. We found that our information practices were great. People really did have access to the information they needed. On the other hand, people were being rewarded for individual contributions and it did not encourage a team approach. We created a new reward and compensation plan that supported both individual and team contributions. We also provided training in team skills instead of just blaming people for not being team players.

· · ·

One morning we were discussing the importance of living our vision moment by moment. As we walked briskly up a hill on a new route, Jim reflected, "You know, Ellie, our walks make a nice metaphor for 'How It's Lived.'"

I glanced sideways at Jim, thinking he was probably onto something. But I was a little too out of breath to respond.

"Here's what I mean," he continued. "We know where we're going. And we've planned the route. But the only thing that is really important is the step you're taking right now. I mean that—literally. The step you are taking right now is the only thing there is. So how you take that step is really important.

Are you present? Do you smell this fresh air? Do you hear the birds chirping? Do you feel the pavement under your feet? Are you living your vision right this moment?"

That took me up short, because actually I had been thinking about making dinner, carpooling, solving a work-related problem, and preparing the paper I was going to write for my course. I hadn't been experiencing the present moment at all. I realized that he was absolutely right. Most of my time was spent thinking about the future and not much actually being in the present.

I responded, "You're right, Jim. Vision isn't really about the future. It's about what you're doing right now."

The rest of our walk was truly amazing as we took in the beauty of the early morning.

A couple of hours later, I listened to Jim's message and was deeply touched.

 Good morning, everyone. This is Jim. I've been thinking about our vision and how important it is for all of us. I want to remind us that the journey is as important as the destination. The only thing that is ultimately real about your journey is the step you are taking right now. That's all there ever is. So it's important to keep your attention on the present. And to be sure that you are acting consistently with our vision, right now, each moment. It's in the richness of the journey where you find life's beauty.

. . .

"I've been thinking about leadership," Jim mentioned one damp morning as we walked briskly in a light drizzle. This morning had been a test of our commitment to exercise because it wasn't bad enough to say we couldn't walk, but it definitely wasn't a beautiful day for a walk.

Jim continued, "I'd like you to react to my thoughts. As I've said before, I think leadership is about going somewhere. When I first took over as president, I wanted to be a good manager. I think I became one. Then I wanted to create a shared vision. Now that we have a shared vision, I'm not so sure about my role anymore."

I said, "So you're wondering since everyone owns the vision, how do the leaders help us?"

"Right. My father was the 'glue'—he had a charismatic personality that held us all together. Now we have a vision, and that is the glue. I don't need to inspire everyone the way my father did—the vision does that."

I ventured, "Well, it doesn't hurt for you to remind us of what's important about the vision and help keep us on course, especially when things are tough."

Jim laughed. "You're right. There *is* a role for me, but it's a different one that I've had in the past. I need to see myself as a servant of the vision, not an important leader who needs to be served.

"I met the chairman of the board of Matsushita Electric when I was in Japan a number of years ago. He was eighty-eight years old at the time. One of the people I was with asked him, 'Sir, what is your primary job as chairman of the board of this great international company?'

"He didn't hesitate. He said, 'To model love. I am the soul of this company. It is through me that our organization's values pass.'

"I really liked that." Jim concluded.

I smiled back. "That really fits for me. One of your jobs, then, is to remind people about what's really important. Another is to help them stay focused on the vision, another is to remove obstacles whenever possible, and another is to encourage them to act.

"Jim, when you shift from a self-oriented perspective, it changes the way you think about leadership. From this viewpoint, leadership is about serving the greater good. There is no room for ego-driven leadership."

"I think you're right. It's my job to serve the associates in our agency so that collectively we can accomplish our vision—not feed my ego."

Later that morning, I wasn't surprised at all to hear Jim's morning message.

Good morning, everyone. This is Jim. I've been thinking about my role as a leader in support of our vision. It's important for me to be a champion for our vision and to help keep it in front of us.

It's my job to help you do your job. In that way, it is my job to serve you, so you can serve your customer. Its not your job to serve upper management. If I ever get confused and give the wrong message, please let me know.

• • •

Jim and I had many conversations about each other's visions. Jim told me he kept his "obituary" in the top drawer of his desk so he could easily reach it. One Tuesday morning he mentioned, "I'm always checking my vision to test whether I'm living it. As you know, the essence of it is to be *a loving teacher and example of simple truths that help myself and others awaken the presence of God in our lives.* Knowing this helps me make decisions. I ask, 'Does this opportunity take me in that direction?'"

I had questions about Jim's vision. I didn't understand what he meant by "awaken the presence of God in our lives." I took that opportunity to ask him outright.

"You often mention God, in your vision, in your daily conversations, and on your morning voicemail messages. Frankly, I have to admit that it makes me uncomfortable. I'm not a member of your religion. In fact, I'm not religious at all in the traditional sense of the word. I'd like to know more about what you mean when you talk about God and what your intentions are."

"Ellie, you always ask the questions that others might worry about but not ask," Jim responded. He paused to consider his response and then continued.

"I believe it's so important that people are connected to a higher power—something bigger than them, something more loving, something more caring. Religion is one way to help people do that."

"So what you're saying is religion can be a vehicle, but not the only one. What's really important is not the vehicle but the experience—to recognize that we're not the center of the universe and are all connected to something greater than ourselves."

"Yes, Ellie. When we put our egos in the center of the universe, we lose the opportunity to connect with something more universal that connects us all. What's important is the experience of connecting to something greater than ourselves, whether it comes through nature, community, or a particular religion. When we make that connection, we shift from a self-oriented perspective to a sense of connection to something greater than the self."

Understanding Jim's views made me more comfortable with his language. And I was reassured to know that Jim accepted my own views.

• • •

"What do you do when something unexpected knocks you off course?" Jim asked me one Tuesday morning.

"What do you mean?"

"I mean, what if your vision is clear, everyone's on the boat and moving full steam ahead, and then something unexpected happens and knocks you off course?" he asked again.

"Why are you asking?" I wanted to know. "Things seem to be going pretty well from my point of view."

"Things don't always work out exactly the way you plan, you know."

His question didn't make sense. It seemed strangely out of context of what was happening. Everything was going well. Everyone in the agency was totally energized by the vision. Jim was a wonderful president and also a wonderful friend. His daughter Kristen had just joined the agency and was quickly learning the ropes. Kristen had her father's engaging personality and everyone quickly grew fond of her. I didn't understand why Jim would be thinking about things not going according to plan. In retrospect, I wonder now whether he was reflecting on his own mortality.

Coincidentally, the subject of getting knocked off course came up at our dinner conversation that evening. Jen told me about a movie she had seen in school about a young man named Terry Fox. I was so intrigued by what she had said that later that evening I did an Internet search to learn more about him. I discovered the story of an amazing young Canadian who understood the power of vision and what happens when you get knocked off course.

While in high school, Terry was named "Athlete of the Year." Shortly after graduation, he discovered he had a malignant tumor; his leg was amputated four days later.

The night before his operation, he read a magazine article about an amputee who ran in the New York marathon. That night, Terry dreamed about running across Canada.

During his follow-up treatment, Terry saw suffering as he'd never seen it before. He later wrote these words in a letter to the Canadian Cancer Society requesting their support:

> As I went through the sixteen months of the physically and emotionally draining ordeal of chemotherapy, I was rudely awakened by the feelings that surrounded and coursed through the cancer clinic. There were faces with the brave smiles, and the ones who had given up smiling. There were feelings of hopeful denial, and the feelings of despair. . . . Somewhere the hurting must stop . . . and I was determined to take myself to the limit for this cause.

He left the cancer clinic with a vision to run across Canada to raise $1 million to fight cancer. There was a second purpose to his marathon—to demonstrate that there are no limits to what an amputee could do and to change people's attitude toward people with disabilities.

At first, Terry kept his vision a secret. He ran in the dark so no one could see him. Later when he felt confident that he could gain their support, he shared his vision with his family and close friends.

Terry trained for fifteen grueling months, until he could run twenty-three miles a day. He took just one day off, at Christmas, and only then because his mother had asked him.

On April 12, 1980, he dipped his artificial leg in the Atlantic Ocean in St. John's, Newfoundland, to begin his run.

Terry became a national hero. He was greeted with cheers as he entered each town. People wept as he ran by, fists clenched, eyes focused on the road ahead, his awkward double-step and hop sounding down the highway.

He'd start before dawn every day, running in shorts and a T-shirt printed with a map of Canada. He didn't hide his disability. His artificial leg was fully visible. Children were curious about his artificial leg. How did it work? What happens when it breaks? He encouraged them to ask questions and always stopped to answer them.

The donations poured in.

Terry ran 3,339 miles, from Newfoundland, through six provinces, and now was two-thirds of the way home. He had run close to a marathon a day, for 144 straight days. But on September 1, 1980, Terry had to stop. He was sick. His cancer had recurred and had spread to his lungs.

He flew home for treatment. And with his family beside him, Terry Fox died on June 28, 1981—one month short of his twenty-third birthday.

Did Terry achieve his vision? I wondered. He didn't complete his run. But then I thought again. His vision wasn't to run across Canada. That was his plan to achieve his vision. His vision was to raise a million dollars for cancer research and to increase awareness about disabilities. In fact, he raised $23.4 million. And his vision didn't end with his death. The Terry Fox Run continues as a yearly event to this day and has raised millions upon millions of dollars.

This must be what Jim was asking about. What happens when unforeseen events throw us off course? Terry wasn't planning on a recurrence of his cancer. It threw him off course, and his plans changed. But his vision didn't.

I shared the story of Terry Fox and what I had learned about vision with Jim. I told him that I thought that when unforeseen events throw us off course, we shouldn't try to get back on course. Instead, we should change our course yet keep our focus on our vision.

I told Jim that I thought we need supporting strategies as well as supporting structures. I had learned the two best supporting strategies from Terry Fox. One was:

Always focus on your vision.

If an obstacle throws you off course, set a new course. Be prepared to change your goals, if necessary.

Change is bound to happen. Unforeseen events are bound to occur. Find a way to describe what is happening as a challenge or an opportunity. The second was:

➤ **Courage of commitment**

True commitment begins when you take action. There will be fears; feel them and move ahead.

Whatever you can do, or dream you can, begin it. Boldness has genius, power, and magic in it.

—GOETHE

I just wish people would realize that anything's possible if they try, that dreams are made if people try.

—TERRY FOX, 1980

Courage

I've concluded that it takes courage to create a vision and it takes courage to act on it.

I really did have a talent for listening and helping Jim synthesize his own dreams into creative expression. I had also helped Marsha, and I had helped my family. But I wasn't doing it for myself. How was I living my dreams through creative expression?

Deep inside I was afraid to admit to myself that if I really acted on my vision, I would have to find another way to earn a living and that might mean losing my connection with Jim. It was a price I wasn't willing to pay.

Meanwhile, the longer I stayed with the insurance agency, the more restless I became. My job there fulfilled a security need but not my deeper purpose. The work I did in the marketing department and the courses I had taken at the community college had helped me further develop my skills and confidence in my writing. However, I lacked confidence in my ability to earn a living through writing.

In addition, my fear of leaving my relationship with Jim was keeping me stuck in a job I no longer found fulfilling.

Especially significant during this time, I made a new friend. I met Brian in one of my writing courses. The first time I saw him, I hardly noticed him because I was so intent on what I was learning. A few weeks into the class, he approached and suggested that we go out for a drink or dessert to discuss our writing assignment. I thought that was a great idea because I really wanted help with the assignment. His intentions were not as simple. He did want to discuss the assignment, but he also wanted to get to know me—which he frankly told me as we sat at the restaurant. I liked him immediately. Something about his directness reminded me of Jim. As I got to know him better, I found that in some ways he was different from Jim. He was a little more fun-loving, for example. He did unexpected silly things that made me laugh. Yet, he treated me with the same respect that Jim did.

Brian was attractive and easy to be with. We enjoyed each other's company. He was clearly interested in developing a relationship with me. I didn't know what kind of relationship I wanted or was even capable of, but I decided it was worth the risk to get to know him better. Although his personality was quite different from Jim's, there was something familiar about the kind of relationship we were developing.

It was several months before I introduced him to my children. As expected, they were wary at first.

I think they were afraid he would upset the stability of our family. But Brian seemed to understand this. He took his cues from the children and never pushed himself on them. Gradually they began to thaw as they saw that he was not a threat.

This must be where courage comes in, I thought. It was becoming clear that my personal vision meant using my talents in creative expression and having loving relationships in my life. Was I now going to take action? For me, action felt like jumping off a cliff. I didn't know where I would land. Would I be able to support myself if I left the insurance agency? Should I allow my relationship with Brian to deepen? I knew what I really wanted. But I was afraid to take the next step.

• • •

I stayed with Jim's insurance agency for over three years. During that time I had participated in developing a shared vision for the agency, as well as a shared vision for my departments. I had worked with my children to create a shared vision for our family and had gained clarity about my personal vision.

I had also developed skills that would help me live my vision, and I had gained confidence to act on it. The clearer I became and the more I shared my vision with my family and friends, the more I found they were willing and able to support me.

One evening Jen said, "Mom, remember the stories you used to tell me at bedtime? They were great! You ought to write some of those stories."

Alex jumped in, "She's right, Mom. You're a natural storyteller."

My children inspired me to take action, and I began to write in earnest. At home in the evenings, I began to write some of the stories I had told the children. But I changed them a bit to include messages about some of the things I had recently learned. I began to imagine writing a book for managers based on the lessons from childhood.

Jim encouraged me to leave the agency and devote myself fully to writing. He promised that if it didn't work out, there would be a job there waiting for me. And, most important, he said we could continue our Tuesday morning walks.

I thought about my vision. It was about truth, not fear. It was about helping people act on their dreams—myself included. It was about allowing, not resisting. Jim, Brian, Jen, and Alex were all supporting me, encouraging me to take the leap. It was time for me to act on my vision.

I created a plan. I saved up enough money to carry us for six months. I had discovered that I could earn some money writing articles for magazines. I decided to take a leave from my job for six months. Within that time frame, I hoped to see whether I could actually earn enough money to live on.

One wonderful day, I gathered all my courage and took the leap.

I knew it would be difficult at first, and it was. We all had to adjust our lifestyles. We no longer ate out in restaurants, and I didn't buy any new clothes for quite a while. We had to learn to live on a sporadic income. When I sold an article, we had money. But there were times when no money came in. Then we had to draw on my savings. We worked hard to make the savings stretch. Jen, who was sixteen now, got an after-school job. Alex, in his first year in college, lived on loans, scholarships, and some help from his father.

Brian was a wonderful support during this time. He read my articles and the various drafts of my book and was very encouraging. It meant so much to have him cheering me on. But there were days I questioned whether I could actually make a living doing this.

Within the six months, though, I knew I had made the right decision. Even though I would probably never be rich or famous, if I lived simply, I knew I would be able to earn a living doing what I loved.

• • •

The year Jen graduated from high school, I had another opportunity to challenge my courage. I had known Brian for two years. We had fallen into a comfortable relationship. Brian was like a rock. He accepted me for who I was and accepted what I gave him, never demanding anything else. I was aware, though, that I held something in reserve. I was afraid I'd never be able to be as innocently vulnerable again as I had been with Doug. Brian seemed to accept that in me.

Unexpectedly, Brian was offered a wonderful job on the other side of the country. He asked me to marry him and go with him. I had no logical reason not to do it. I was in love with him, my children were no longer living at home, and I had a job I could do anywhere. The only reason not to do it was the biggest reason: I was afraid. Marriage would be a huge commitment. I hadn't done such a good job the last time I had tried it. Things with Brian were great the way they were. If we got married, I thought it might ruin everything.

Brian confronted me. "I love you, Ellie. I know you love me. And I know you hold something back. It's time to let go. We deserve to really be together."

I told Brian I needed more time. He told me there wasn't more time. He was moving, and he wanted me to come with him.

I hadn't seen Jim for a while. Our Tuesday morning walks had become infrequent. But I called him and asked whether he'd go for a walk with me that morning.

I told Jim about Brian's job offer and his desire to get married. I told him about my dreams and my fears.

Jim asked me simply, "Are you in love with him?"

I responded immediately, "Yes," and then added shyly, "I'm in love with him, and I'm afraid."

Jim smiled softly. "Ah, Ellie. I remember the day I met you seven years ago. What a bright light you were and still are. You've made my life richer. But in my marriage, Carolyn and I have experienced a kind of love that is only available in the intimacy of commitment. Brian is offering you this gift, and it is a perfect fit with your vision."

Walking there so comfortably with my dear friend Jim, I realized that through our relationship, I had grown and was now open to the possibilities of a loving, mutually respectful commitment. I was drawn to what he described as the intimacy of commitment. I had thought I could never totally trust again, but I realized that I did trust Jim and I could trust Brian if I would allow myself.

I thought about my vision; it included loving relationships. I realized that by holding back on Brian, I had been limiting myself—limiting the possibilities of living my vision fully. At that moment my last wall went down, and I knew that I would have the courage to marry Brian.

From Success to Significance

In the five years that followed, I was able to apply the principles of vision that Jim and I had learned together. I published a book for managers, titled *Mother Goose Management*, that took lessons of childhood stories and showed how they illuminated the principles of vision.

My marriage with Brian was strong and fulfilling. He helped me stay connected with what was deeply meaningful and true. We had our ups and downs, but we were always able to work things out through the intimacy of our commitment.

One day I was cleaning out my files, and I came across the folder that contained Jim's voicemail messages that I had transcribed over the years. As I flipped through them, I came across one that made me pause.

 Good morning, everyone. This is Jim. Last night I was at a party with people that I haven't seen for a long time. It was really fun.

> *I saw an old friend who had helped me get*
> *started in the business. I told him about our agency's*
> *vision and thanked him for the part he played in*
> *our success as a company and in my life. I could just*
> *see the beam and smile on his face.*
>
> *The question I have for you today is, is there*
> *anybody in your life who was there for you, whom*
> *you haven't thanked lately? Maybe you haven't*
> *given them a hug. Have you kept your "I love you's"*
> *up-to-date?—with your parents or relatives, or*
> *friends, or people who were there for you way back?*

It had been a long time since I had been in touch
with Jim. I decided to write him a letter and tell him
how much he had meant to me—how much he had
influenced my life for the better. My letter came from
deep within my heart and was very personal. I thanked
him and told him I loved him. I didn't mail the letter
right away. I wanted to make sure it expressed exactly
what I wanted to say. I waited a week, reread the letter, and then mailed it.

• • •

Three days later I got a call very early in the morning.
I picked up the phone as I finished pouring my cup of
coffee.

"Ellie, this is Kristen. I wanted to let you know
that Dad is in the hospital. I know he would want me
to call you."

"Is it serious?" I asked.

Kristen hesitated. "I'm afraid it is, Ellie. It's his heart. He had rheumatic fever as a child and had heart damage. He had been told he would never live this long, but he didn't believe it. He never told anyone about this except Mom."

I couldn't speak. After a pause, Kristen continued, "He'd been feeling ill for about a week. At first, he didn't mention it to anyone. You know how he is. When he got worse, he went to the doctor and was told he had the flu. He spent the next couple of days in bed. But he kept feeling worse, and then last night we had to rush him to the hospital."

"How bad is it?" I managed to say through the lump that had suddenly appeared in my throat. I couldn't believe what I was hearing. Jim always seemed so strong . . . somehow invincible.

"There's really not much they can do for him," Kristen responded, her voice cracking for the first time in our conversation. "He's in the ICU, and the doctors didn't expect him to last the night. He's not conscious, but he's still with us this morning."

I hung up the phone and just stood there—completely stunned. How could someone with the biggest, strongest heart I'd ever known have a problem with his heart? It didn't make sense. All I knew was I needed to see him again. One last time. I needed to tell him in person what I had written in my letter. I needed to hold his hand. I needed to tell him I loved him, even though I'm sure he knew that. I didn't even know whether my letter had reached him.

I hung up the phone, scribbled a note to Brian, grabbed my pocketbook, and headed straight to the airport. I was on the next plane out.

The whole time on the plane I closed my eyes and concentrated on Jim. I tried to feel his heart beating. I tried to send the strength from my heart to his. I did my best to stay calm and reached out to him with my spirit.

I called Jim's house from the airport. Kristen answered the phone.

"Don't go to the hospital, Ellie. Come to the house, OK?" she said gently.

That's all she said. I didn't ask any questions, and she didn't volunteer any information. So, I knew. But I also didn't know. It wouldn't be true until someone actually said it. And no one had said it yet. Numbly, I sat in the back of the taxi as I headed to Jim's house.

I rang the doorbell, and Kristen answered. She didn't say a word. She just put her arms around me and started to cry. And my tears finally spilled out. The truth had been spoken, without words. I couldn't fathom it. But I knew Jim was dead.

• • •

After the funeral, we came back to the house. People were everywhere. Carolyn and Kristen were busy talking with relatives. I didn't know what to do with myself. I didn't really know anyone there well, and I didn't feel like small talk.

I wandered down the hall toward the bathroom, passed Jim's study, and was immediately drawn in. It didn't even occur to me that this was a private space. I so strongly felt the need to connect with something of Jim. I walked to his desk, sat down, and looked out the window for a long lonely time. This was the desk that Kristen had found Jim's obituary in—his vision for his life. I glanced down, and there on his desk, still open, looking like it had just been read, was the letter I had sent him. I breathed a sigh of relief. He had gotten my letter. He knew what I was doing and how I was making my vision a reality. He had heard me tell him one last time how special he was to me and how much I appreciated him. I picked up the letter and read it again—thankful that I had taken the time to write it and that he had been able to read it before he died.

There was another sheet of paper under my letter. I had picked it up by mistake. It contained some sketchy notes in Jim's handwriting. As I read what he had written, I realized that these were his notes for what would have been his next morning message.

I studied the words:

- moving from success to significance
- when you're ready to do that, it's time to think about giving back to your community
- the vision is about more than just you
- we're all in this world together

I could almost hear him speaking, "Good morning, everyone. This is Jim." And it seemed as though his last message was for me. As I sat in the silence of his study, his words sank in, and I began to imagine what it would mean to expand my vision to my community. It would mean teaching others about the power of vision.

And so, I said good-bye to Jim and thanked him for his last gift—the encouragement to continue on my journey—to recognize that life is a journey that doesn't end with "success."

Epilogue

The mark of a true visionary leader is that the vision continues beyond the lifetime of the person who articulated it. Just as the vision of Martin Luther King Jr. continues to inspire and provide direction for so many of us, Jim's agency continues to thrive under Kristen's leadership. She has taken it in some new directions—possibly ones that Jim wouldn't have. But the underlying values remain. And it continues to be an energized workplace with a vision closely held and shared by all.

Jim's insurance agency was just featured in a popular business magazine. In the article, one of the employees interviewed said:

> We are part of an industry that many people love to hate. But our customers, the customers of our agency, don't feel that way at all. In fact, they respect us and are extremely loyal. We have incredibly low turnover, and we've grown continuously. How can that be? How can we be doing so well in this industry? It's because every single one of us knows and is committed to our vision—

our purpose, our values, and our picture of the future. These aren't just words on some document filed away in an office. They are part of the daily conversations that guide our every moment here. If a stranger walked in off the street and asked the question "Why does your company exist?" he would get the same answer from any person he asked—from the receptionist, to the agents, to customer service, to the custodian. The same would be true if he asked, "What purpose do you serve?" or "What values guide you?" or "What's your picture of the future?" Every single person in our company would give the same answer.

• • •

As for me, I'm still working on my vision of moving from success to significance. I've discovered that as we move full steam ahead toward our vision, our vision expands the closer we come to it. My vision has expanded to include my community. I've realized that on this planet, we are all part of one community, and we all need to assume responsibility for creating a shared vision.

I learned that the images we hold in our minds have a tremendous impact on the realities we create. I am concerned that there are so many images of destruction in movies, on television, and even in electronic games that children play. In contrast, there are so few images of what peace looks like. When I ask most people to describe what world peace looks like, they use vague terms. However, they are able to give quite vivid descriptions of what a post–World War III world would look like. I've put a bumper sticker on my car that says, "Visualize world peace." And I look for any opportunity I can to help people create positive images for our planet.

Moving from success to significance means understanding that everyone must benefit from your vision. If your vision does not benefit those who are not part of it, at least it must not cause them harm. Thus, I discovered another underlying principle of vision:

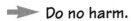 **Do no harm.**

People have asked me whether Hitler had a vision. Understanding this final principle, I now know that the answer is no. It might have looked like a vision to those who would benefit from it: the reestablishment of Germany as a leading nation and the exaltation of the Aryan race. However, harm was done to those it did not include. Many suffered horribly as a result of this false vision.

A vision must take into account the larger community that is touched by those who share it. With that in mind, I have expanded my vision to include a larger and larger scope. I'm confident that as my vision continues to expand, I'll recognize other opportunities as they arise, and I will have the courage to act.

The reason I wrote this book is to help others understand the power of vision and how to create a vision for their company, their work, and their lives.

Thanks, Jim. Your vision was to have *made the world a better place by having been there*. It is. And I continue to move full steam ahead, my friend.

Acknowledgments

We would like to thank several people for their support and contributions.

Steven Piersanti, president of Berrett-Koehler Publishers, for his faith in the book and excellent editorial advice.

Drea Zigarmi (co-author of *Creating Your Organization's Future*), **Marshall Sashkin,** and **Joan Brandon** for influencing Jesse's early thinking during her doctoral studies and for helping identify some of the important concepts presented in our book.

To those who allowed us to help in your journey, we thank you and extend our admiration. You have had the courage and the tenacity to make your vision a reality. Specifically, we would like to recognize **Jim Lorence** of The Stanley Works, **Nancy Maher** of TJX, and **Dan Miglio** of Southern New England Telephone, courageous leaders with whom we have had the honor to work closely over a significant period of time and watch them go the distance. Through working with you, we learned more about vision in action.

163

Chris Brunone, Steve Gottry, Marye Gail Harrison, Judd Hoekstra, Fay Kandarian, Gail Katz, Louise Klaber, Michele Kostin, Donna Mellen, Ros Melowicz, Barbara Rosen, Janice Rotchstein, Judy Schlossberg, and Rabbi Alan Ullman for their detailed and insightful feedback on early drafts of the book.

Dottie Hamilt and Marsha Wilson for always being there when we needed help and for coordinating activities; Judy Albietz for her support and good advice; and Joan Stoner for her enthusiasm and editing expertise.

Early pioneers in the field of vision and leadership for their studies and insights: Peter Senge, Charles Kiefer, and Peter Stroh for describing visionary organizations and the concept of structural integrity; Warren Bennis, Marshall Sashkin, Barry Posner, and James Kouzes for their studies of characteristics of visionary leaders; Robert Fritz for his thorough explanation of the concept of creative tension; Mary Parker Follett for her contribution to the law of the situation; and Joanna Carver Colcord, author of *Sea Language Comes Ashore*, for information on the expression *full steam ahead*.

And to our families: To Jesse's husband Larry Zemel and children, Michael and Noah—for their constant love, support, and encouragement, especially during the many hours of absence while writing this book. To Ken's wife, Margie, for her wisdom, love, and sharing their vision.

About the Authors

Ken Blanchard, co-founder and chief spiritual officer of The Ken Blanchard Companies and chairman of The Center for FaithWalk Leadership, is the author or co-author of over thirty books, including one of the best-selling business books of all time, *The One Minute Manager,* and the giant business best-sellers *Raving Fans, Gung Ho!, Whale Done!* and *Empowerment Takes More Than a Minute.* Credited with twelve best-sellers to date, his books have combined sales of more than thirteen million copies in twenty-five languages.

Ken also co-developed Situational Leadership® II—among the world's most practical, effective, and widely used leadership programs on the market today. In demand as a keynote speaker, he has addressed numerous gatherings of Fortune 500 companies as well as leaders from around the world.

Ken maintains a visiting lectureship and also serves as trustee emeritus at Cornell University, where he received his Ph.D. He has received many honors, including the prestigious International Management Counsel's

McFelly Award, putting him alongside such honorees as W. Edwards Deming and Peter Drucker.

Ken and his wife, Marjorie, and their two children, Scott and Debbie, all remain active in The Ken Blanchard Companies, which is headquartered in San Diego, California.

Jesse Stoner, president of Seapoint Center and a consulting partner with The Ken Blanchard Companies, is a highly regarded and experienced consultant, executive coach, and author. The primary focus of Jesse's work for the past twenty years has been helping organizations create a sustaining shared vision.

Jesse has worked with organizations worldwide to help them create a compelling vision, identify the strategies to capture it, and ensure that it is lived. She also works with individuals to clarify their personal visions. She has worked within a wide range of industries, such as retail, hospitality, manufacturing, pharmaceutical, health care, government, education, and nonprofits.

Co-author of *Creating Your Organization's Future*, a program that helps teams develop a shared vision for their team, department, or organization, Jesse has also authored several training materials on teamwork as well as numerous journal articles.

Jesse holds advanced degrees in psychology and a doctorate in organization development from the University of Massachusetts. She lives in Connecticut with her husband and children.

Services Available

The Ken Blanchard Companies

The Ken Blanchard Companies is a global leader in workplace learning, employee productivity, and leadership effectiveness. Building on the principles of Ken's books, the company is recognized as a thought leader in leveraging leadership skills and recognizing the value of people in order to accomplish strategic objectives. The Ken Blanchard Companies not only helps people learn but also ensures that they cross the bridge from learning to doing.

The Ken Blanchard Companies helps leaders apply the principles of *Full Steam Ahead!* through a program that helps a leadership team develop a shared vision for their business unit or the entire organization and to identify the strategies to achieve it. In addition, The Ken Blanchard Companies conducts seminars and provides in-depth consulting in the areas of teamwork, customer service, leadership, performance management, and organizational change.

To learn more about *Full Steam Ahead!*, other books by Ken, or other corporate services, visit the Web site at www.kenblanchard.com/fullsteamahead, or browse the e-store at www.kenblanchard.com/estore.

The Ken Blanchard Companies
125 State Place
Escondido, CA 92029
Phone: (800) 728-6000 or (760) 489-5005
Fax: (760) 489-8407

Seapoint Center

Seapoint Center, under the leadership of Jesse Stoner, helps people create a compelling vision of their desired future, to identify the levers to create momentum, and to establish the processes to sustain their efforts for their work and/or personal lives.

Other services include training for leaders who want to learn how to facilitate the process of creating a shared vision in their organization. The focus includes authentically using oneself as an instrument of change, creating one's own vision, the process for creating a shared vision in an organization, and principles for supporting the journey from vision to reality.

Seapoint Center also facilitates large-scale high-involvement meetings where a large group or an entire organization comes together for real dialogue, to define its futures and solve real problems.

For more information, please visit the Web site at www.seapointcenter.com or contact:

Seapoint Center
PO Box 370053
West Hartford, CT 06137-0053
Phone: (860) 521-8080

Creating Your Organization's Future
The *Full Steam Ahead!* Field Guide

Creating Your Organization's Future is a powerful results-oriented program that facilitates a group through the steps described in *Full Steam Ahead!* It is designed to assist a leadership team with creating a vision for their department or organization and identifying the strategies to make it a reality.

Step 1: CREATE SHARED VISION
Agree upon a *significant purpose* and *clear values* for your team, department or organization. Next, create a description of a *picture of the future.*

Step 2: HONEST DESCRIPTION OF CURRENT REALITY
Examine your current realities in relation to your vision. Identify the strengths and weaknesses of your organization in relation to your ability to achieve your vision. *Holding the vision and being honest about the present.*

Step 3: STRATEGIES TO MOVE FORWARD
Identify greatest opportunities to leapfrog forward. Identify *supporting structures* needed. Develop *bridging strategies* to guide your movement forward.

Step 4: PLAN FOR INVOLVEMENT
Develop a plan to involve the rest of your department or organization in shaping the vision, to identify roadblocks and to develop specific plans for action: *how it's created* and *how it's communicated.*

Step 5: PERSONAL COMMITMENTS
Make individual commitments to begin to live the vision now: *how it's lived.*

For more information on this program, contact The Ken Blanchard Companies, 125 State Place, Escondido, CA 92029, Tel. 800-728-6000, 760-489-5005.

Empowerment
Takes More Than a Minute
Second Edition

Ken Blanchard, John Carlos, Alan Randolph

These expert authors explain how to empower the workforce by creating a supportive, responsibility-centered environment in which all employees have the opportunity and responsibility to do their best.

Paperback, 145 pages • ISBN 1-57675-153-8
Item #51538-415 $12.95

The 3 Keys to Empowerment
Release the Power Within People
for Astonishing Results

Ken Blanchard, John Carlos, Alan Randolph

This user-friendly action guide expands on the three keys to empowerment presented in *Empowerment Takes More Than a Minute*. It provides managers with clear advice, effective activities, and action tools to create a culture of empowerment.

Paperback, 200 pages • ISBN 1-57675-160-0
Item #51600-415 $12.95

Hardcover, 200 pages • ISBN 1-57675-060-4
Item #50604-415 $20.00

Managing By Values

Ken Blanchard and Michael O'Connor

The authors provide a practical game plan for defining, clarifying, and communicating an organization's values and ensuring that its practices are in line with those values throughout the organization.

Hardcover, 140 pages, • ISBN 1-57675-007-8
Item 50078-415 $20.00

Audiotape, 2 cassettes/3 hrs. • ISBN 1-57453-146-8
Item 31468-415 $17.95

Berrett-Koehler Publishers
PO Box 565, Williston, VT 05495-9900
BK Call toll-free! **800-929-2929** 7 am-9 pm Eastern Standard Time
Or fax your order to 802-864-7627
For fastest service order online: **www.bkconnection.com**

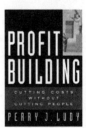